The
Compleat Gardener

The Compleat Gardener

By Molly Hackett and Georgianna Taylor

The Missoulian,
Missoula, Montana

Cover and book design by Kathleen Herlihy-Paoli.
Watercolor painting on the cover by Marion Lavery,
for information on her work contact
Sutton West Gallery, 121 W. Broadway, Missoula, MT 59802.

ISBN 0-9634679-4-8

Printed in Montana on acid-free recycled paper.

Our thanks to all the gardeners who asked the questions.
You made this book possible.

Contents

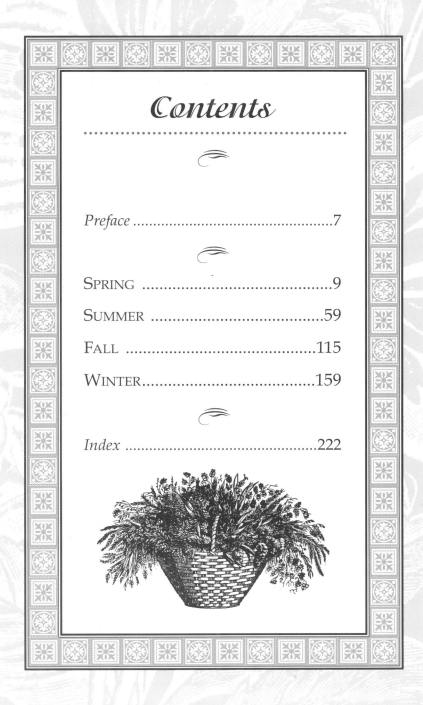

PREFACE

or everyone who thinks he doesn't need another gardening book, we are here to tell you you are wrong.

If there's anyplace in the world with a climate less hospitable to gardening than western Montana, it must be Antarctica. We have it on good authority that it is even easier to grow things in Siberia than it is here.

This book is a collection of some of our *Dirty Fingernails* columns which appeared in the *Bitterroot View*, a *Missoulian* section. Our object in writing the column is to provide localized information on gardening—indoors and out. Most of the information in national magazines, while often perfectly good advice, is written for somewhere else and doesn't pertain to our vicious climate.

From time to time we give unsolicited advice, but most of the column consists of answers to actual questions posed by readers in the area.

We decided to do the book because readers got tired of cutting the columns out of the paper and we got tired of looking things up for them again.

We chose the name *Dirty Fingernails* and our motto, "Never trust a gardener with clean fingernails," because we are both hands-in-the-mud home gardeners with years of experi-

ence. We both are Master Gardeners and are always trying to learn more about gardening and growing better things.

We do not wear gloves in public, and are not ashamed to let our cracked fingers and grimy cuticles hang out of our slightly soiled sleeves. (Can any gardener resist pulling those last two dandelions from between the flagstones, even on the way to church?)

If anyone out there has a gardening question or problem, don't hesitate to write to us at the *Missoulian*, 500 S. Higgins Ave., Missoula, Montana, 59801. We're still at it.

Spring

CONTINUED NEXT PAGE

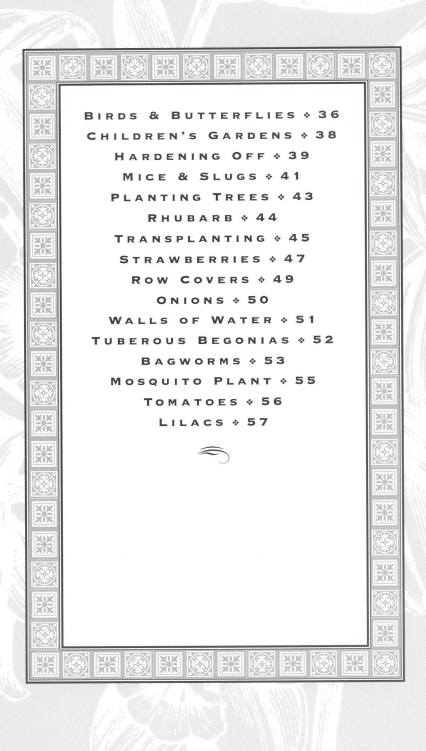

When preparing ground for a new garden bed, how deep do I need to dig? From one quarter I heard you must double-dig new planting areas, but from another I heard that digging deeply just brings weed seeds to the surface where they can grow.

 It depends on what's there already and what you plan to plant. Annuals, which include many flowers and most vegetables, have shallow roots that occupy only the top 6 inches of soil. If they have that much good stuff, they don't much care what's below. Also, with annuals, you don't have to worry about getting every goody into the soil the first year because you can always do more next season.

Perennials, by and large, have much longer roots and they do care what's down there. Also, you won't be digging them up and adding nutrients next year. For them, you need to dig deeper — at least a shovel-depth, however deep that is. We haven't measured our shovels, but figure it's about 9 inches.

Many perennials will have to be dug and divided in three or four years, but others, like peonies and asparagus, can live longer than you do. For those things you should dig even deeper and augment the soil, since it will probably be your only chance.

This is true on an even larger scale for trees and shrubs, which need a very wide hole at least two shovels deep.

Planting advice has changed in the past few years. They used to say to take the soil out of the hole and replace it with a nice, loose mixture. Many of the trees looked very good for the first few years, but after five to 10 years, they began to decline. When they were dug up, it was discovered that the roots couldn't get past the edge of the original hole and had just had to circle around, like being in a big cement pot.

Now the experts say not to be that nice to your new trees and shrubs. It's better to say, "OK, kids — tough it out."

Dig up your soil and take out the big rocks, but don't add manure or soil from elsewhere. Put the plants in the soil

11

you've got. They might take longer to get established, but they will be tougher and more at home in the long run.

While you're down there in the hole, scatter around a little superphosphate or bonemeal and mix it with the bottom layer of soil to encourage root growth. Although our soils usually have plenty of phosphorus, much of it is not in a form available to plants.

Do not put in any other type of fertilizer. You run a great risk of burning the roots and you will be stimulating top growth at the expense of the roots. Woody plants, especially, have trouble supporting much leaf growth before their roots get well established.

If you have quack grass (haven't we all?) you must be sure to get rid of it when creating a new bed. When you till quack grass rhizomes, you just cut them up so they can make lots of new plants quickly. In three weeks you will have a luxuriant crop of quack grass and you will never see the garden again. Take the sod off entirely and turn it upside down on the compost pile.

You will have some weeds the first year—there is just no help for that. Every time you stir up the soil, you will get some new ones.

 We have just completed our new home and I'm anxious to start forming garden beds. How can I prepare beds for rich, loose soil?

 You may have to deal with what the contractor has left you, but by and large, this is a good area for making flower beds.

Most of our soils are sandy loams—the best soil you can get. The sandier your soil gets, the faster water runs through it. The finer the soil particles, the less water penetration you get—real clay doesn't let the water through at all.

Early spring is a good time to start digging. The soil is

moist, and the weather is good. When you start digging down, you can tell where topsoil ends and subsoil begins because it will be a different color—usually lighter. Topsoil can be anywhere between half an inch and 10 inches deep.

Most gardeners will be satisfied with merely adding organic matter to the soil. Lay out your beds and dig up the area, removing rocks ("soil particles" 3 inches in diameter are considered a little coarse for flower beds) and any chunks of concrete, two-by-four trimmings and PVC pipe scraps deposited during construction of your house.

Leave any old, dead vegetable matter. Do not leave quack grass roots or you will have a quack grass jungle before your first seeds come up.

You want to provide your flowers with about 8 inches of good, loose soil, which is about one shovel-depth. Unless you have problem soil—drainage problems, for instance—it is hard to rationalize double-digging, but we'll explain that in a minute. Usually you just need to dig in a good amount of organic matter.

We like Eko-Compost, Milorganite or the equivalent, and as for amount, we recommend buying two bags more than you can afford. Although peat moss is not ideal, you can use it if you are sure you mix it with the soil extremely well. When peat dries out, as your beds will do several times during a season, it sheds water and is hard to dampen.

If your beds are going to be too wide for you to reach everything from the edge, put in paths right away. Once you have your soil dug up, you don't want to have to step on it and pack it all down again.

After a rain, go out in the evening with a flashlight and relocate any earthworms you find in your yard into your flower beds. Worms are a gardener's best friend and will do a lot of your cultivation for you. If your yard doesn't have worms, go to other people's yards and sidewalks after a rain and adopt the worms you find. If you are worried about getting arrested during this process, look for signs advertising fishing worms for sale and buy yourself dozens and dozens.

Start right now to collect your raw materials for a compost pile. Make a pile of any grass, leaves and garden debris you rake up in your yard and add all your kitchen garbage *except* animal waste. Do not include any grease, meat or bones, because they will make your compost pile smell terrible, attract all the dogs within miles and repel neighbors within the same distance.

Do include fruit and vegetable peels, egg shells, coffee grounds, terminally limp celery, overripe pears, and so on. If you are ever going to double-dig, this is the time to do it, and you never have to do it again. People who double-dig more than once are in it for the exercise, which is considerable.

Start by spreading a tarp along your flower bed. Dig out a hole one shovel deep and two shovels wide, piling the topsoil on the tarp. Then dig another shovel-depth and put that into a wheelbarrow to be hauled off and deposited where soil quality is less important. Put half the soil from the tarp back into the hole and add lots of organic goodies to the rest before returning it to the hole. Proceed down the bed, one shovel-width at a time, putting half the topsoil into the previous hole, hauling off the second shovel-depth and mixing organic matter into the rest.

Your soil will not be as good this summer as it will be in future years. Building good garden soil is a gradual process. You won't ever have to dig up the whole bed again—just keep adding organic matter every spring, digging areas where you plant.

14

My mom always used a lot of bonemeal in the garden, but it seems like it is rarely used any more. Does it help or not?

Bonemeal used to be considered one of the really important sources of plant nutrition. However, about 10 years ago we starting reading that to be effective, bonemeal had to be fresh and that the steamed bonemeal being marketed was no good. Probably only the most die-hard organic gardeners still use it. The reason it fell from favor is not that gardening has changed, but that bonemeal has changed. There are many industrial uses and the best bone-meal is now used for such things as gelatin, chicken feed and pharmaceuticals. Only the stuff not good enough for industry is bagged up and sold to gardeners.

Bonemeal formerly contained 10 percent to 12 percent nitrogen and 5 percent to 10 percent phosphorus, but recently scientists bought and tested some and found it to be 0 percent to 5 percent nitrogen and 0 percent to 10 percent phosphorus. If you really want to use bonemeal, it is best to grind your own, which is possible, but you need to be highly motivated.

I know it's time to apply fertilizer, but every time I look at a bagful, I get confused. What do my plants need and what's the best way to provide it?

Here is a short course in fertilizers for non-chemists: The first three elements plants require are carbon, hydrogen and oxygen, which they get from the air in carbon dioxide and water.

The next three necessary are nitrogen, phosphorus and potassium, which are often represented by their chemical symbols N, P and K. They always appear in the same order on fertilizer labels.

The numbers on a fertilizer bag represent the percentage

by weight. If it says 16:20:0, the fertilizer contains 16 percent nitrogen, 20 percent phosphorus and no potassium. If it said 4:5:0, the ratio of nitrogen to phosphorus would be the same, but you would need four times as much fertilizer to get the same amount of nutrients.

Nitrogen contributes to leaf production and is especially good for grass and leaf crops such as lettuce. All plants need it because they must have leaf surfaces to photosynthesize. Being water-soluble, nitrogen is quickly washed away by irrigation and rainfall.

Phosphorus promotes fruiting and strong root systems. It is very slow to disappear and doesn't go much of anywhere. If you put it on top of the soil and don't mix it in, it may never reach your plants' roots at all. When worked in properly, phosphorus remains available in the soil for several years.

This is an area where you can usually forget about adding potassium at all. In the semiarid soils of the Intermountain West, we have plenty already.

When you read a magazine article or fertilizer sack, it's important to remember that the information is probably meant for somewhere else. If you read that wood ash is good for the soil, that message is definitely not for you. Wood ash contains potassium and makes the soil more alkaline. Our soils are alkaline enough already.

Unless you are trying to grow things like rhododendrons or holly, you usually don't have to worry about the acidity-alkalinity — the pH — of your soil. You must be very dedicated to grow acid-loving plants.

There are several other minerals plants need, but in such small amounts that they are referred to as "trace nutrients." Organic fertilizers and good inorganic mixtures include these.

"Organic" means the stuff came from animal or plant sources. These include manure and compost and such things as bonemeal, bloodmeal, fish emulsion and sewage sludge.

"Inorganic" fertilizers are just as natural as organic ones, but they came from non-living sources. Organic is not automatically good and inorganic is not automatically bad.

A plant cannot tell the difference in where its nitrogen came from, but it certainly can tell if it's in a form the plant can use.

There are many reasons you might opt for organic fertilizing. First, organic fertilizers are more likely to contain the trace minerals. Second, manure and compost are a whole lot bulkier than inorganic, pelleted fertilizers and contribute good things to the soil's humus. Third, it is a lot harder to put on too much.

Granules from a bag are very concentrated and it is easy to burn your plants. If you are broadcasting inorganic granules, one pellet per inch is a lot. You definitely don't want to make it look as if it just snowed on your garden.

There are a couple of organic fertilizers that need not be used here. Greensand can be avoided because it adds potassium. Rock phosphate will not decompose in your soils; therefore, its phosphorus never becomes available to your plants.

The best thing you can put on your garden is lots of compost. Gardeners call it "brown gold." With compost, as with chocolate chip cookies, homemade is best, but store-bought is still pretty good.

When you use manure, be sure it is "aged" at least a year before it goes on the garden. Fresh manure may contain undigested disease organisms. If you use horse manure, you will probably get a good crop of weeds because, unlike cows, sheep and chickens, horses do not digest the seeds they eat and they come out just as viable as they went in.

WARNING: You must beware of Tordon. It is a very efficient herbicide that has been used a lot lately on knapweed. It is environmentally safe, in that it goes directly through animals without hurting them. However, what makes it good for killing knapweed makes it death on gardens. It is very long-lived and continues active in the manure from animals who have ingested it on fresh plants or hay. How long it remains varies with conditions, but Tordon can last 10 years in the soil. It is not destroyed by heat.

Before you get manure, make sure it does not come from animals who ate plants sprayed with Tordon. If you are suspicious, put a bunch in some soil and grow one tomato plant. If it grows twisted leaves, looks sickly or dies, do not put that manure on the rest of your garden.

In the flower beds, fertilize perennials now and forget it. Annuals may do better with a little bit once a month throughout the season.

Vegetables that grow most of the season—corn, tomatoes, onions and melons, for instance—prosper with several applications of fertilizer. Things that are mostly leaves like a little nitrogen early, just to get them going. Don't bother your legumes—they are busy making their own nitrogen.

 You have indicated we do not need more potassium in this area. My soil tests say that I need as much potassium as nitrogen. They indicate a need for nitrogen, 4 percent; phosphorus, 14 percent and potassium, 4 percent. They also reveal a medium amount of humus and a nine pH. Isn't this too alkaline?

Yes—a pH of nine is too alkaline to grow good vegetables. You can try to raise the acidity of your soil by adding ammonium sulfate or agricultural sulfur. Or you could move your garden.

You can never take anything we say as absolute gospel—it may not be true for your area. And you can always find atypical places. You may be trying to garden in an old bog, in which case your soil would be unusually acidic. Or you may have a shallow layer of clay, which would sub-irrigate all summer.

You cannot garden by formula. However, if you are having a problem that could be attributable to nutrient deficiency, by all means have your soil tested. If you don't have knapweed and your quack grass is looking sickly, you have a problem and need to find out what's happening with your dirt.

You can have it tested by a lab or do it yourself.

There are all kinds of home test kits. The simplest just shows the pH. Electronic ones are more expensive, but more accurate.

You can mess up soil tests very easily if you don't follow directions exactly. It is vital to have a representative sample of your garden's soil.

There is a whole lot of art, luck and uncontrolled nature in gardening. Every year something is going to do especially well and something is going to do poorly, and it's never the same thing two years in a row.

 What kinds of herbs can I grow here?

 There are dozens of herbs — both annual and perennial — that do pretty well in the soil and climate of the northern United States.

In general, herbs — especially the Mediterranean ones such as marjoram, oregano and rosemary — need good drainage. The mints are about the only ones that like to be wet. Chervil needs partial shade, and some others will grow there, but most herbs are sun-lovers.

There are many that deer don't like, which is good news for many gardeners.

Beginning with annuals to grow from seeds, there are at least 10 different kinds of basil. If you want to cook with it, get large-leaved varieties. The compact plants with small leaves are for decoration. Lemon basil has a lovely flavor. Sacred or holy basil smells a bit like huckleberries and goes well with fruits.

You can start basil inside and set it out later, but don't plant seed outside until the second week after you expect the last frost. It hates to have cold feet.

Chervil is delightful in salads and is one ingredient

you'll want when you make your own *fines herbes* mixture with parsley and chives. It tastes like a mild tarragon and looks like parsley. It reseeds itself very nicely.

Upland cress tastes like watercress, which doesn't grow here unless you have a warm-water spring. You need to plant upland cress every week or so because it goes to seed amazingly fast.

"Bouquet" is a good dill to use for seed or seedheads. Try "Fernleaf" or "Tetra" dill for leaves to chop into vegetables or salads. Plant seed directly in the garden because dill does not appreciate transplantation.

Fennel looks quite a lot like dill, but has licorice-flavored leaves and seeds. It does not take kindly to transplanting, either. This common fennel should not be confused with Florence or carosella fennel, which have thick stems and are grown as vegetables.

Lemon mint is really a bee balm, *Monarda citriodora*.

Although they are perennials in milder climates, marjoram, oregano and rosemary must be grown as annuals here and should be started from seed indoors, early.

If you plan to cook with your oregano, don't buy any seed unless it says it's "true Greek oregano." Anything else is likely to be *Origanum vulgare*, which is wild marjoram and very ornamental, with lavender or pink flowers, but no flavor. Culinary oregano is white-flowered.

Parsley is really a biennial, but in its second season grows only a few leaves before bolting, so plant either curly or flat varieties as annuals.

Garlic and shallots are annual herbs grown for their bulbs instead of foliage or seeds. Just buy the bulbs sold in the produce department of the grocery store, separate into cloves and plant 5 inches apart and half an inch deep. Plant garlic and shallots with your earliest garden plants if you have never grown them before. Planting garlic in the fall and overwintering it will get you larger bulbs the next summer, though.

Common perennial herbs you can grow from seed

include chives, lavender, sage, thyme and the mints, including catnip.

Thyme is marginal here, so be prepared to replant after a hard winter. Lemon and ordinary thyme are the ones to cook with, but there are also several nice ornamentals.

Spearmint and peppermint do well here and are good, but some of the flavored mints aren't all they are cracked up to be.

Plant mint where you can get at it to dig, pull, trim and clip to prevent an unfriendly takeover. Planting mint in heavy shade holds it back somewhat.

Less common perennials you could try include burnet, bergamot, hyssop, lemon or lime balm, lovage, French sorrel and sweet woodruff.

You might like to try chamomile, even if you don't want it for medicinal purposes or tea. It is interesting because, although it grows quite tall out in the middle of the garden, if you plant it between your flagstones and walk on it occasionally, it branches and stays low. Its fragrance is released by the feet that brush it.

The interesting thing about sweet woodruff, other than that it is used to make May wine, is that it doesn't smell until after it is dried.

True French tarragon—the kind to use in cooking—does not set seed, and the plants must be taken from cuttings. Don't buy tarragon seeds. They are from Russian tarragon, which has little flavor. To overwinter successfully, tarragon needs winter mulch and some protection for the first few years.

You could plant your herbs among your flowers or vegetables, or make an herb garden. The latter can be very casual, with an English country feeling, or extremely formal, with fancy planting designs and artistically trimmed plants.

Put a good edging around your herb garden to keep the grass from creeping in and the herbs from creeping out.

Although the herbs are virtually pest-free, they are very attractive to beneficial insects.

An old wives' tale has it that herbs like poor soil, but that is not strictly true. They will grow in poor soil, but do better with adequate nutrients. Don't fertilize too much if you're growing for flavor and aroma because it dilutes the essential oils.

 I'm getting anxious to poke some seeds into dirt — isn't it time to plant anything yet?

 Yes. Late winter is the time to start perennials and the annuals that take a relatively long time to grow, like pansies, petunias and snapdragons. Seed packets should tell you how far ahead to plant each kind.

By March 1 you could plant a tomato or two if you are willing to transplant it a few times. You can start your broccoli and cabbage now if you have walls of water to protect them when you set them out.

It really pays to buy special seed-starting mix. "You get what you pay for" applies to starting medium as well as seeds. You won't need a bushel. You can get a dozen seedlings to transplant out of a single 2-inch pot of starting medium. If you plant two or three seeds in each cell of a six-pack, you can usually get a good seedling out of each cell.

Plant 50 percent too many. If they all make it, give some away or save only the best to plant out.

Fill your containers to within a quarter-inch of the top and dampen the soil mix. A good mix takes up water easily and holds moisture longer without getting soggy. The soil moistens easier if you use warm or hot water. Put seeds on top of damp soil.

For vegetables, use two or three seeds for each plant you want; for flowers, four or five seeds. Don't use too many or you will have to thin out a lot, which is a traumatic experience for most plant-lovers.

Cover vegetable seeds twice the depth of the seed. Some flowers need light to germinate and will not be covered at all, while others may require a light soil cover. Peat moss is a good thing to cover seeds with because it has fungicidal properties and fungi are a major enemy of seedlings. Use cardboard to cover pots of dark-requiring plantings.

Cover your planted containers with plastic to cut down on watering. (Greenhouse flats come with plastic covers.) Most plants germinate at temperatures warmer than those at which they later grow comfortably. However, putting them on top of the refrigerator is no longer a valid suggestion. Modern refrigerators' better insulation and the bottom-venting systems mean the plants are no warmer on top than they would be on your counter top.

If you see mold on your soil, it doesn't mean anything, but if you see mold on your seeds, it means they are not alive. A seed coat has a component that prevents mold growth, so if a seed is moldy, it is no longer viable.

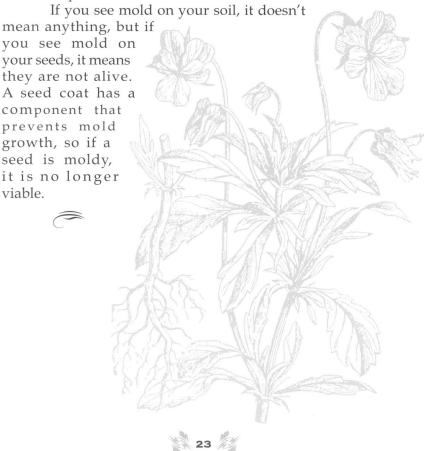

I want to start my own garden plants from seed. When do I start? How can I keep the seedlings from getting spindly? Should I start them in small or large pots? What about grow lights?

These questions came from several different readers, but since they all concern seed-starting, we'll tackle them together.

It is easy to tell when to plant. Just look on the seed packet. It will tell you how many weeks the variety takes from planting to transplanting outdoors. Simply count backward on the calendar from the time it's safe to put that crop out. Don't add extra time. If it says six weeks, eight will not be better and 10 won't grow you a bigger plant. Unless you have a lot of experience, don't try to jump-start things that way. It's not like the days-to-maturity where we add days because of our climate.

You must plan to re-pot at least twice. It is important that you not let the root space get cramped. By the time you are ready to set them out, your plants will be in fairly large pots — 4-6 inches. You need to plan where you are going to put them all because they are going to have to be inside, at least at night, until a week before they can live in the garden.

Spindly plants have had too much warmth for the amount of light they have received and are growing taller in an effort to get light. Give your seedlings the most light you can and try to keep the temperature low.

Seeds germinate best at 70 or warmer, but most seedlings grow best in the 60-degree range. Cool and sunny is a hard combination to achieve in the house.

A windowsill will probably be your best possibility. You can multiply the amount of light your baby plants receive by putting a reflector behind them. A three-sided screen of cardboard covered with aluminum foil helps a lot with light.

Grow lights are the best solution. With them, you don't need any daylight at all. You get better growth with the special, wide-spectrum fluorescent tubes, but regular fluorescent lights do a pretty good job.

You can set a regular shop light on cement blocks and put your trays of plants underneath. Or you can make an expand-able-contractible light stand from PVC pipe.

Under lights, keep your baby plants' leaves within an inch or two of the lights. It is easier to move the plants up and down than to move the lights. Georgianna almost squashed a third of her houseplant population when she tried to raise her four-tube grow light.

There are many choices of containers in which to plant your seeds. Expandable peat pellets are easy, but they are small and you do need to put them in pots later. Peat pots also are easy because you plant the whole thing. Little pots made of newspaper work like peat pots and are plantable. Old flower-pots are eminently recyclable. Milk cartons and plastic contain-ers are fine, but be sure you poke holes in the bottoms. Several types of plastic trays, both Styrofoam and hard plastic, are made just for seed-starting.

If you are a serious seed-starter, you might consider in-vesting in a little wooden appliance for making small newspa-per pots, or in a steel press for turning out 2-inch soil blocks.

When starting seed, be sure you have about 2 inches of depth to allow for the development of a good root system. You don't need much horizontal room.

You can plant an entire package of seeds in a 4-inch pot and, once they are up and fairly well-established, transplant them into a large tray or into 2-inch pots. Whatever the con-tainer, you want space equivalent to a 2-inch pot per plant for most of its growing time. If you just start one plant per pot, it saves you one transplanting. Don't start a single plant in a pot larger than 2 inches.

When starting things like squash and cucumbers, which do not transplant well, start them in peat pots so they can be set out whole and their roots not be disturbed. Plan on no more than four weeks from planting to setting out.

You will discover that plants you start from seeds are

smaller than ones you would buy in six-packs or pots, but they also are healthier and will grow into nicer plants. If you buy plants, it's better to transplant them once before setting them out.

You want to set out plants while they are in a vegetative state—still growing. If a plant's roots have had to stop growing out and down because they were restricted by pot size, it will not be as healthy a plant and will not bloom or produce as well as one whose roots have not been stymied.

Flowers need to be put out before they have blooms on them. When they are, their blossoms will come on sooner than the second flowers of plants bought already in bloom.

....

hen finally the weather looks as if spring may yet arrive, gardeners begin to think there may be a point to planting seeds after all.
One of the first things to consider, of course, is your potting medium. It is fairly important to start seeds in sterile medium to avoid fungal diseases. You want the soil to hold water, but you also want air spaces and good drainage to promote healthy baby roots.

You can't just plunk seeds into a pot of garden soil and expect great results, because the air and texture are not right.

The easiest thing to do is buy sterile growing mix. If you want to make your own, be sure you include something like compost or garden soil to provide nutrients and air spaces, and to hold water. Add something non-absorbent, like perlite or coarse sand to provide drainage. Peat moss also helps to hold moisture.

One year at this time, about to sterilize homemade potting soil, we were at the stage of "I don't want to bake all this stuff," and we moved to sterilizing with bleach. We have since stopped because some of the seedlings were not happy with that soil.

Since then, we have been pouring boiling water over potting soil. That only sterilizes the top half inch of the soil, but to start seeds you don't need any more depth. By the time the plant has roots long enough to go lower than that, they are strong enough to resist diseases that might be in the medium.

Put the medium into the container in which you will plant, pour the boiling water over it and allow it to cool to room temperature before planting your seeds.

We discovered this in a book by Norman C. Deno, "Seed Germination—Theory and Practice," published in 1991. Deno, a retired professor of chemistry at Penn State, published the results of his experiments, most of which were directed toward germinating difficult native plants.

He has six systems for breaking seed dormancy and encouraging germination. He has been trying them all; he knows and explains why he gets the results he does and he has found things that work for him. Much of his book is a long list of times and temperatures for specific seeds.

Problems with soils for germination mostly involve fungi. Wireworms will attack seeds, but are not likely to be running around live in your potting soil.

Sterilizing soil with heat is, at best, an inexact science. You may be told to give it 1 hour at 350 degrees, or 15 minutes at 300 degrees; do it wet; do it dry; put it in a paper bag; cover it; don't cover it.

Remember, if you get stuff hot enough to kill the bad creatures, you are going to kill the good micro-organisms, too. Also, if it gets too hot or stays hot too long, you will end up with a whole lot of carbon and no nitrogen. Organic material breaks down when exposed to enough heat.

It has been reported that 7 minutes in the microwave will sterilize soil, but many experts do not recommend this method because they feel it may change the mineral balance and pH of the soil.

Of course you can buy sterile potting soil, but it only stays sterile as long as its environment remains sterile, which probably does not include sitting around open in your garage or potting shed.

Be careful with your watering. Seeds germinate best in

damp, but not wet, conditions. The wetter the soil, the more chance you have of starting a fungus colony. Damping off, the situation where healthy young plants suddenly keel over at ground level, occurs when a fungus ruins their plumbing system and water can no longer travel up the stem.

Starting medium does not have much in the way of nutrients, but nutrients are not required for germination or for a week or two after. You can either add a good pinch of long-acting fertilizer to the medium before planting, start fertilizing a week or so after the plants come up or transplant into a soil containing nutrients.

Many seeds do not need any light to germinate. The packets of varieties requiring light for germination will tell you not to cover the seeds. Otherwise, germinate your seeds out of the sun and move them to a sunny spot after they are up. Check daily for their little green noses poking through.

Vegetables are the easiest plants to start from seeds. If you've never tried it before, tomatoes are a good place to start. Flowers are a little trickier, but you might try marigolds or cosmos. Start nasturtiums in peat pots so they don't have to be transplanted.

If you are looking for more challenge, try starting perennials. They germinate just as well, but take longer to grow. You can grow from seed some plants that are difficult—or expensive—to get elsewhere. Also, you can plant the seeds any time from February through June and the plants will be big enough to set out by the end of summer, to bloom next season. Columbine and foxglove would be good to start with.

Spread the seed thinly and be prepared to keep the soil moist for quite a while—perennials take a long time to germinate. The days to germination listed on the package may be very inaccurate—either way. A thyme whose packet said it would take 30 days to germinate came up in six on Molly's windowsill.

Some seeds are picky about temperature and need to be kept cool. The seed packet should tell you an acceptable range.

Styrofoam meat trays make excellent saucers, once you have a lot of pots of seedlings sitting around. Several pots will fit on one; they protect the underlying surface and you can feel virtuous about recycling something.

Suggestion: When you water your baby plants, try using an old liquid detergent bottle. You can easily aim the stream, and it's gentle and won't knock the seedlings over.

 My seedlings are popping up—how soon do I have to worry about transplanting them?

 If you planted the seeds in separate containers, they need not be transplanted soon, but only thinned. As soon as they show their first true leaves, thin the plants to three in each little six-pack pocket. Then, once they have two well-developed true leaves, thin to one plant per section.

The first leaves you see are "seed leaves" and do not look like the leaves the plant will develop later.

With annual flowers, you can leave the plants in the original containers until the top growth is bigger than the containers. Annuals' root growth is shallow and small. Just be careful not to leave them in the container until they make flower buds—put them in bigger pots before that happens, to prevent root crowding.

Perennials and vegetables need to be put in bigger pots sooner. It matters more how deep the container is than how wide. Vegetables and perennials put down long roots, and you want to provide as much depth for roots as you have height in top growth. Once a plant is 2 inches tall, it is time to take it out of its six-pack or 2-inch pot and give it more room.

Expect your cucumbers and tomatoes to get to that point faster than your daisies and delphiniums. Perennials grow quite slowly.

Do not try to save yourself the time and trouble of an additional transplanting by going directly from a six-pack to a giant pot. If there is too much soil with no roots in it, it is likely to get waterlogged, which encourages anaerobic bacteria and fungus colonies. Transplant from six-pack to 3- or 4-inch pots and from there to 5- or 6-inch pots. By that time, the plants should be ready for the garden.

When you transplant, put some fresh potting soil in the bottom of the new pot to give the plant's roots a place to grow down; set the seedling on top of it and fill around it to the same level.

Tomatoes are a notable exception. You can bury quite a lot of the stem, and the plant will grow roots from the buried stem.

Other plants can be put a little bit deeper if their stems are weak and skinny—but only a quarter to a half-inch. If you bury any more stem than that, it is likely to rot.

Do not pack the soil down when you transplant. The seedlings need lots of air spaces in which roots can thrive. We recommend settling the soil in the pot by holding it firmly in one hand and clapping it soundly on the side with the other hand. Then, when you set it down, give the pot a firm rap on the table.

Have your seedlings' soil moist when transplanting so that the most soil possible will remain on the roots. If you

must separate seedlings, handle them by a leaf, not by the stem. They can survive a squashed leaf, but not a squashed stem.

When potting up seedlings, especially vegetables, it is of primary importance not to allow the plant's growth to be slowed down. The most common way of slowing growth is not to re-pot soon enough, allowing the roots to get crowded. So if you don't have time to transplant, make time.

I planted a six-pack of seeds and a week later only one section had sprouted. What did I do wrong?

 There are many possible answers. The first one is that you have done nothing wrong at all. Seeds germinate irregularly, and even if all the seeds in all six little pots were from the same package, it is not unusual for some to come up faster than others.

Maybe one corner of the six-pack was a little closer to a heat source or accidentally got more or less water than the rest. Don't throw out the others — in another week they may all be up.

Water is obviously a possibility — if seeds are too wet they will still germinate, but not as well, and at a slower rate. If they are too dry from the outset, they will not germinate. If they have been kept moist until they have committed to germination — a couple of days — and then allowed to dry out, they will die.

Lift your six-packs once a day and give them a drink when they start to feel light. If you are afraid you won't be careful about watering, err on the side of too much.

It is possible that some of your seeds were planted deeper than others. If some were covered a sixteenth of an inch deep and others a quarter, they may all come up, but at widely different times.

When starting seeds indoors, don't cover them as deeply as you would when sowing them directly in the garden. Outside, the depth is needed to keep them moist and to protect them from cold and sudden changes in the weather. In sterile starting mix, if you plant seeds too deep, the sprouts may run out of steam before they reach the surface.

Temperature makes a big difference to seeds' germination. The rule of thumb is 70 degrees, which is normal house temperature under ordinary conditions. But a cold snap may cause your indoor temperature to fall slightly and a drop of just a few degrees can have a major effect.

Your seeds themselves may be the problem. Not all seeds

are created equal. A company may have produced a bad batch. Maybe they weren't mature when they were harvested. If that was the case, they will have to sit there in the moist soil and finish maturing before they germinate.

If your seeds are old, especially if they have not been carefully and correctly stored, they might germinate, but not as well as fresh ones.

To try to figure out what went wrong, dig up your seeds and examine them. If they are just gone, they rotted. Rotten seed may have been dead when you got it — you always have a few dead ones in any seeds you get.

If you rummage around in the dirt and find seeds that still look like they did when you planted them, try giving them different conditions — warmer, cooler, more dampness or less. Some seeds need dark to germinate and should be covered with cardboard or layers of paper. Some flower seeds need light — uncover the seed and sow it on top of the soil.

The reason we can tell you all these things that can go wrong is that they have all happened to us at one time or another. Every single spring we plant seeds and we think every one of them is going to come up. They don't.

You have to believe in the miracle, but no matter how optimistic you are, not all of them are going to make it.

The general rule for seed starting is to germinate warm and grow cool, so keep the planted pots out of the sun; once the plants are up, quickly put them into very good light and cooler temperatures.

At this point, water is absolutely critical. Your baby plants no longer have the protection from disease and fungi formerly provided by their seed coats, and there are all manner of enemies waiting to attack those new roots.

The soil must be kept damp, but cannot be soggy. Every so often, turn a pot over and take out some of the dirt to see just how wet it is down there.

The lower the temperature, the slower the plant's respiration rate and the less water it needs.

Once your plants develop their first pair of true leaves—not the seed leaves that emerged first—it is time to transplant or thin them. If you planted in a six-pack you can snip off all but the two healthiest seedlings in a section and a week later cut off one more, leaving a single plant in each little pot.

Cut, don't pull, the unwanted seedlings. Embroidery or manicure scissors will work. Pulling is likely to damage the tender roots of the plants you are saving.

It's hard to imagine how many roots—including root hairs—a plant can have. One horticulturist reported that a single 20-inch rye plant had 400 miles of roots in its two cubic feet of soil.

If you have planted your seeds over a large soil area rather than a pinch-to-a-pocket in a six-pack, separate the seedlings very gently. A grapefruit spoon makes a handy tool. Handle the tiny plants only by the leaves, not by the stems.

Poke a hole in the new soil with a ballpoint pen and carefully insert the seedling. The soil should not be packed down too hard. Just tap the pot on the counter to settle the soil, or poke gently with a fingertip.

• •

The National Gardening Association got 10 testers around the country to start the same peppers in three different ways—plastic pots, peat pots planted intact and peat pots torn open at transplant. They learned that, without exception, northern gardeners got bigger plants and more peppers from the plastic pots, while their least satisfactory results were the peat pots. Southern gardeners had exactly opposite results, with the best crop from peat pots and the worst from plastic. The torn peat pots came out in the middle. Experts had no satisfactory explanation immediately, although a few were silly enough to try.

We have two large plants of creeping phlox, 3-5 feet in diameter, which were planted in 1984. The last couple of years, they have developed dead spots along the edge and in the middle. Could it be they don't get enough water, need fertilizer, need to be separated? Or do they just deteriorate with the years?

 Your plants probably don't have any problems. What you describe is partly natural for phlox and partly attributable to age.

You asked at a good time. Now, before perennials start to grow, is the time to deal with problems. It gives them the whole season to reorganize themselves.

Your plants don't sound sickly. Just cut out the dead spots and they will look better right away.

Any time you prune, you encourage new growth, so even if you have holes in your carpet of phlox big enough for the ground to show through, they will fill in by midseason.

Creeping phlox grow two different kinds of stems — one that flowers and the other that puts down attachments and forms new plants. Sometimes a stem may get so long that it doesn't get enough nutrients and it dies and you cut it off.

This is not a fussy plant. It doesn't need an enormous amount of nutrients and is drought-tolerant. As with any plant, you can check to see that it's getting enough water by digging down near the plant to make sure the soil is not dry to a depth of more than an inch.

If an older plant is not blooming as profusely as it used to, you can give it a sprinkle of fertilizer, but don't get carried away.

The dead spot in the middle suggests age in the parent plant. Perennials typically form a doughnut shape in the center as they age, which is your cue to divide them.

The kindest and most effective way to do this is with clean, vertical cuts with a sharp shovel, rather than digging up the entire root ball and trying to pull it apart gently.

This may sound violent, but you will actually damage

fewer roots. Just cut the plant in chunks, replant what you want and give the rest to the neighbors. Keep divided plants moist if you have a dry spell. Most perennials are fairly deep-rooted and the divisions will not have had a chance to re-establish their deep roots.

There is no set rule for how often a perennial needs to be divided. Some require division every two or three years and some can be left alone practically forever. If perennials get so crowded that they don't do well, divide them, even if they haven't formed the telltale doughnut shape in the center.

If you didn't cut your perennials to 2 or 3 inches in height last fall, quickly do it now. The top is dead and only the root and crown are alive. An inch to an inch-and-a-half is the shortest you can go without fear of damaging the buds that have already formed or without cutting into the crown, and thus providing access for disease.

There are quite a few perennials, like lavender, which have semiwoody stems. These should be cut down to 6 inches or so in height. If you don't, you will wind up with tall brown stems with green leaves on the top.

Now is also the time to fertilize perennials. They like nothing better than an inch of compost on top of the soil around them — under the "petticoat," in the case of your big creeping phlox.

Perennials are such satisfactory plants. You don't have to buy more every year and you can keep a few treasured ones for a long time. You can get a tiny bit from someone special, grow it for a few years and then share it with someone else.

 I saved my poinsettia and now it looks terrible. It's leggy and growing new leaves at the top, and the flowers are bleached out. What do I do?

 Cut your homely, gangly plant back to about 6 inches now. If you don't, it will soon grow through the ceiling. It will look pathetic for a while, but it really doesn't mind and will reward you by growing back much bushier. Don't worry if you cut off almost all the leaves.

In late summer — August is just right — you will need to repeat the major surgery.

Cut the plant *way* back — just above the first fully formed leaf on each stem. It will look pathetic, but within a week, it will have begun to grow. You are just moving the growth from high up to lower on the plant.

Unless you prune a poinsettia unmercifully at least twice, you will end up with a tall, gangly plant with no leaves on the bottom half. It will be ugly and hard to take care of. When it begins to bloom, it will become even more top-heavy, and you are likely to get up some morning and find it bent in half.

 Please tell us what kind of flowers to plant to attract butterflies and hummingbirds. And hurry. It's nearly time to plant!

 The two basic things in attracting both birds and butterflies are water and a variety of plants. Different bugs like different plants, and you want to provide a wide choice of insect populations to draw birds. Even hummingbirds like tiny insects on the wing, as well as nectar.

In a healthy garden ecosystem, most insects are neither harmful nor beneficial, but simply coexist with your plants. Because harmful insects are the smallest percentage in a garden population, when you increase the number of bugs, you are increasing the good ones more than the bad ones.

When you are purposely attracting birds and butterflies, it is important to use integrated pest management. This does not mean that you use no chemicals, but that you concentrate on physical methods of control and use chemicals only as a last resort. Even then, use agents that will not harm the species you seek to draw. You don't want to annihilate the birds' food supply, and some insecticides will harm the birds and butterflies directly. Insecticidal soaps, oil sprays and Bt (*Bacillus thuringiensis*) preparations are safe to use.

It is interesting to note that the red, yellow and pink flowers which generally smell better to humans are pollinated by flying insects, while funny-smelling white ones are more likely to be pollinated by bugs like beetles.

Now, what to plant. A rule of thumb is to "provide edges." This means that bird populations are thickest where one ecosystem flows into another — where trees become bushes, where bushes border on grass and where lawns run into flowers.

Plant both vegetables and flowers, and plant as wide a variety as possible to give lots of homes for lots of kinds of things. Using mulch also provides homes for bugs.

In planting flowers, plant for the longest possible continuous bloom. This means spring-flowering bulbs, followed by lilies and daylilies. Perennials bloom early and annuals later.

By the time hummingbirds arrive, most bulbs have finished blooming and when annuals are at their peak, the hummers are starting to leave, so concentrate on your perennials. However, plants attractive to hummingbirds also are attractive to hummingbird moths and butterflies that stay later.

If we were to choose the three top flowers to attract hummingbirds, they would be fuchsia, columbine and delphinium. Others include clematis, foxglove, bee balm (monarda), most pinks (including sweet william), nicotiana, monkey flower, catnip (if you can stand to have it around), coral bells, iris, lupine, penstemon, phlox, sage, scabiosa (pincushion flower), verbena, yucca, flowering onion, fall-blooming aster, globe thistle, lavender, lychnis (Maltese cross), fleabane and goldenrod.

In general, butterflies prefer clusters of small flowers to single large blooms. Butterflies, hummingbirds and other nectar-lovers look for tube-shaped flowers.

To attract birds other than hummingbirds, you need to provide places to perch, roost and nest, which means trees and bushes, as well as insect populations to feed on. You will probably not be able to attract seed-eaters except as the winter feeding season begins, when they will appreciate sunflowers and the seeds and berries of trees and shrubs.

Is Your Child Interested in Gardening?

The American Horticultural Society did a study on what children want to grow. They found out that kids don't really care that much about growing vegetables. They said they wanted flower gardens.

Not only that, they wanted some special things in their flower gardens. They wanted things that smell good, flowers that are unusual, a variety of different flowers and flowers that are pretty. And they wanted their gardens to have secret places.

That sounds nice to old people, too. Even if your garden grows in half a barrel, you could grow a shy, good-smelling, pretty, unusual flower like a primrose, dwarf stock or sweet woodruff in a secret place under a protective columbine, Shirley poppy or sacred basil, although a secret place big enough to sit in would be a soul-satisfying thing for a gardener of any age.

Are there things I can do to maximize my seedlings' chances of surviving the move outdoors to the garden?

 The process of easing the transition is known as "hardening off," although in Montana, it might better be called "toughening up."

If you take the tender babies you have grown — or the expensive babies you have purchased — directly out of your house and plunk 'em into the garden, many will simply turn up their toes and die and others will be crippled for life.

The inuring process must last at least seven days — 10 won't hurt. On the first day, take the little plants outside and make sure they have shade. They probably can stand up to two hours of sunshine, but not in the middle of the day.

Always protect seedlings from the wind. You can set them in a box that is as tall as they are. Also, choose a spot for them on the sheltered side of a building. Around here, that usually means on the east side. Even after planting, your young plants will have to be protected from wind until their roots have become firmly established in the ground.

Gradually increase the amount of time your plants spend in the outside world until, at the end of the week, they are out all day. Do not leave them out all night for the first several days and be sure to bring them in if there is a chance of frost.

The plants will probably need more water outside than they did in the house because of the increased air circulation and the sunshine.

We are believers in floating row covers, and this is one place where we recommend them. If you drape a sheet of row cover over them, your young plants will be able to spend more time in the sun and will not dry out as fast.

You also could build yourself a lath frame that will serve the dual purpose of providing shade for your plants and keeping your hands busy until it is time to plant your seedlings in the garden. The ideal ratio for such a frame is 50 percent wood and 50 percent air.

Remember, these plants think they have been living in Hawaii. Introducing them to our outdoor climate gradually will help prevent the jet lag that could kill them.

 My late seedlings are about to take over my house. Is it safe to set them out now that we have reached the last average frost date?

 The answer is, "Yes, but with reservations."

The tender things should be safe now, but nobody can guarantee we won't get a frost — or several frosts — later. It's a fact of life in Montana. So you must be prepared to protect the wimpy plants if you or the weatherman suspect a frost may arrive.

Beware of possible cold night temperatures if the day-time temperature has not gone over 70 degrees and the skies are clearing at evening. In those conditions, cover your tender plants. Row covers make good frost protectors. Plastic makes the least satisfactory covering.

Warm-season plants often benefit from mulch to heat things up. Black paper makes good mulch for such crops as melons, tomatoes and squash.

Plastic is fine if you have a way to get water under it. Clear plastic heats the soil the most, but weeds flourish under it and you must be prepared to lift it to weed.

As you prepare to set out your plants, cover the soil with the mulching material and cut slits or X's in which to plant the seedlings.

Green peppers like a moderate climate and, like lilies, want their faces in the sun and their feet in the shade. We have had the best luck by coddling the green peppers — surrounding them with old windows or walls of clear plastic to cut the wind and cold drafts. They also appreciate a cooling, thick, organic mulch, such as straw or bark.

Something is eating my seedlings—from the shiny paths in the flowerbed, I assume it's slugs. How can I get rid of those disgusting creatures?

 Slugs have no apparent redeeming social value. They eat a lot and they reproduce rapidly, a feat each one accomplishes all by itself.

Slugs feed at night and spend their days in a damp, shady place, like under a board or a low-growing plant, or in cracks in the ground, which is where they overwinter. They may well make their home in one area, but go out to lunch.

If a plant is just a baby, a slug will eat the whole thing, so if you have entire plants disappearing overnight, suspect slugs. The slime trail you mentioned is conclusive evidence.

Favorite meals for slugs include peas, lettuce and strawberries (the fruits) and most flowers growing in shady places.

If a plant is too big to finish in one meal, the slug will just eat holes in it.

Remedies include traps, baits and brute force. You have probably read and heard about beer traps where the slugs come to drink and drown. There are very complicated instructions to make fancy ones; you can buy them ready-made or just sink a tuna can in the garden soil.

There have been many tests—some more scientific than others—to discover which brands of beer slugs prefer. They seem to be connoisseurs, opting for the most expensive brew if given a choice.

In California, a test used foot-square boards with 1-inch crossbars on the bottom—the sluggish equivalent of cathedral ceilings. Slugs crawled under at night and could be collected each morning.

The experimenter painted these all different colors and learned that his slugs preferred green ones, with red coming in second.

The rind of half a grapefruit or orange set upside down, an inverted flower pot or a nice, wide board will all attract slugs.

But with any trap you have to collect in the morning the ones you lured in during the night. It is not a pleasant task to dispose of a dish of drowned slugs in stale beer, either.

There are copper-foil barriers that work on the slime, giving the slug a shock if it tries to cross the foil. However, the barrier must be placed all the way around the area to be protected and does nothing to discourage the slugs already living within its borders.

Commercial slug baits are really not very useful. Their active ingredients are mostly metaldahydes, to which slugs quickly adapt, and you end up with a strain of slugs immune to the poison.

You can spread things around individual plants to act as barriers — wood ash, salt and diatomaceous earth. The University of California tested these and says all of them work, although not everyone agrees with the University of California.

Molly has found diatomaceous earth quite effective around strawberries. Just remember that none of these barriers works when wet and must be replaced after rain or watering. Salt must be put on something secure to keep it off the ground and removed before it gets washed into the soil.

A good part of the value one gets from the use of slug traps is the entertainment of catching the critters. Experienced gardeners don't trap — they go out in the dark with a flashlight and kill slugs.

Two rocks are effective, a rock and a stick, a gloved thumb and forefinger. You can also encourage toads to live in your garden and feast on the slugs.

You don't have to do your whole garden. Just take your flashlight to the areas where you have observed damage and let it go at that.

An added advantage to this method is that you will discover that there aren't as many of them out there as you thought.

Slugs are flush at the beginning of the season and again when it gets cool and damp in the fall, but are not usually much of a problem during the warmer, drier weather of summer.

What advice can you give someone about to plant her first tree?

 Rules for planting trees and bushes have changed in the last few years, and it is a much easier task now. They used to say you had to dig a $20 hole for a $5 plant. That meant to dig a hole much bigger than the root ball you intended to put in it and to add all sorts of good stuff to the soil before filling up around the tree or shrub. The experts have had a change of heart.

Now the plan is to dig a hole just capacious enough to hold the root ball, and not to augment the soil at all. The theory is that the new plant has an easier time becoming adjusted to the real-world environment of your yard's soil if you don't pamper it at first with a bunch of goodies.

It is a fine idea to use tablets of root stimulator in the hole or to water with a vitamin solution, but do not add fertilizer when you plant a tree or bush. In fact, don't fertilize at all for the first year. Fertilizers are likely to burn tender roots and may even kill the tree.

It is important to settle the dirt well around the roots of a newly planted tree. Fill the hole halfway, pour in a bunch of water, let it drain and repeat. This helps maintain soil contact with roots, which don't deal well with air pockets. Any root that is left in an air pocket will die.

Your planting job is not finished for two weeks more. The thing you have planted has very limited roots, and hair roots are all but nonexistent. Therefore, for the first few weeks, you need to water it every day or two, then begin tapering off. This applies even when you are planting native species that you don't plan to irrigate at all later.

Another change is in pruning. Experts used to tell you to prune trees and bushes at planting time, but now they recommend cutting only broken or obviously dead roots or branches. Then wait to see what dies and cut that off. This does not apply to fruit trees, which you begin shaping immediately by pruning.

I want to plant some fruit trees, but need to know which varieties of plums, pears and apples are best-suited to this area.

Although not all sorts of plums do well here, most cultivars of prune plums are pretty good. Pears are a problem because they are so susceptible to fire blight. We haven't found a variety that can resist the disease. Many early-season apples will bear lush crops in Montana, though perhaps not every year. Apple varieties to avoid are long-season ones like Granny Smith. The apples won't always have time to ripen before they run out of summer weather. Worse yet, the tree won't think it's time to harden up its growth and go dormant by the time freeze up comes. It will still be making leaves and tender twigs that will all die. Before many years, so will the tree.

Why can't I get my rhubarb to do anything? I thought anybody could grow rhubarb anyplace.

We can't say for sure what your problem is, but our best guess is that it has to do with the soil. Since it mostly does grow so easily, nobody bothers to study it much. We suggest you try moving your rhubarb to a location that is as different as possible from where it has been.

Rhubarb failure is not due to a lack of a pink thumb. Molly had the same problem you report when she lived in another home, but now her rhubarb is thriving and productive. Every few years she carves away big chunks of the crown and puts them in the compost pile — where they grow.

To start rhubarb in your garden, plant a crown division. Do not harvest any at all the first season. The second, pick very sparingly. By the next year, if all goes well, it should be ready to provide a full crop.

Pick your stalks by pulling, not cutting. Harvest after the leaf is completely unfolded, but before it gets old and haggard. Never pull more than half the stalks. Stop harvesting when stems start coming up skinny.

If you have a healthy rhubarb plant that's blooming, cut the blossoms off. If you let it go to seed, it will provide you with 100,000 little rhubarb plants.

In choosing a variety, try a very green kind if you are having trouble. The redder the stems are, the prettier the product, but the greener they are, the heavier the production.

Rhubarb is a very heavy feeder and does well on organic stuff like manure or compost applied a couple of times a year.

Divide your crown when it produces only thin stalks. This is major, industrial-strength work that may require a spade, shovel, digging fork and butcher knife. A Pulaski is very useful, if you have a forester handy.

 When is the best time to transplant lilacs from one area of my yard to another? In fall, before the leaves drop or in spring, before leaves appear, or any time? Should I root-prune early and transplant later? I have eight or nine small bushes in an out-of-the-way spot which I'd like to move, but I'd hate to kill them in the process.

If they are common lilacs (*Syringa vulgaris* or any of its cultivars) and fairly small, moving them should not pose much of a problem.

Common lilacs love it here so much that they are practically indestructible. You see them blooming cheerfully in the middle of a big nowhere at a spot where a homestead used to be—no irrigation, no nothing. Fancy varieties are less hardy.

There are arguments for moving the bushes both in fall and in spring. Those who favor the fall feel it lets the plant grow roots through the fall and early winter until freeze up and have them in place and ready to put on a good season's growth next season. The spring movers feel they are giving the shrub the entire summer to make roots and a good crop of leaves to gather nutrients for the roots to store. There is no single right answer.

We try to move our shrubs in spring. We believe fall is a little more iffy in this climate because the plant must have time to grow roots before it can survive the winter, and here you can't really plan on when the ground will freeze and put a stop to that process until spring.

If you do move your bushes in the fall, you must be sure that they stay wet through the winter. It is well to mulch them heavily the first winter.

If you do your lilac transplanting in spring, do so before the buds open, which means early — as soon as you can get the job done without employing a bonfire or blasting powder to make a hole in the ground.

As for root-pruning, it won't hurt anything. French lilacs, which don't produce many suckers, would be most likely to benefit from it.

For those unfamiliar with the process, it is done by cutting a circle around the shrub about a shovel deep and a foot out from the trunk.

The object is to cut through some of the big long roots, encouraging the plant to grow many new ends (apical tissue) which produce a lot of fine roots near the trunk.

An important advantage to moving your own bushes, as opposed to planting new bare-root ones, is that you can keep the dirt on the roots, saving many of the hair roots.

Water the soil before digging the plant, enough so the dirt will cling and not enough to be mucky.

Have the hole ready in the new location so you can get the shrub back in the ground immediately.

Once you have removed your lilacs, you need to decide

whether or not to prune them. For a spring move, wait and let the lilac tell you whether it wants to be pruned. For a fall move where you have obviously lost a whole lot of roots, you would be wise to cut back the top some. If the plant has a high proportion of leaves to roots, it will lose water faster through transpiration than the roots can bring it in. However, if the disparity is not great, the photosynthesizing leaves make it easier for the roots to grow fast.

Whenever you move your bushes, give them a dose of vitamin B root stimulant to reduce transplant shock.

 What is meant by a "day-neutral" strawberry?

 June-bearing strawberry varieties bloom and fruit just once—in the spring. Everbearing varieties go through the process twice, giving you two heavy crops with a few stragglers in between. Day-neutral plants give you what amounts to three crops, with some overlap. They do this because they don't care, in their blooming and fruiting process, how many hours of sunlight each day offers. Hours of sunlight are what triggers the cycle in the other berry types.

Day-neutrals were developed originally by Dr. Royce Bringhurst, who began crossing cultivated everbearing strawberry varieties with wild ones in the Wasatch Mountains of Utah in the late 1970s. He was trying to breed a strawberry that would bloom and bear at any time during the growing season.

The first two varieties available to home gardeners were Tristar and Tribute. The consensus has been that Tristar is best and toughest in our climate. There are newer varieties, but neither of us has tried them. We are content with our Tristar patches.

If you are new to growing strawberries in this area, we recommend that you not start with June bearers. They are the easiest to find, produce the biggest berries and grow lovely

plants, but unless you have a very protected spot, the blooms will almost surely freeze in some years. They bloom only once, usually in May, and if those blossoms freeze, they will not re-bloom until the next spring, when they may just freeze again.

Another decision you must make when planting strawberries is whether to keep them three years or only two. There are gardeners who will say they have had the same healthy plants for years and years, and that probably is true. However, after three years, production declines so drastically that it is impractical to keep them. If you decide to keep your plants three years, let some runners develop, but not more than one plant per stem. After the first plantlet develops, chop off the rest of the runner. Plant the plants 2 feet apart and let the first daughter plant grow.

If you let all the runners grow, you will still get berries, but production will be cut. Also, if you plant any closer than 9 inches, you will notice a marked reduction in the size of your berries.

If you decide to replace your strawberries every other year, plant them 9-12 inches apart and remove all the runners. Let the plants grow and bear for two seasons and then replace them.

When you take out old strawberry plants, replant in a new area, giving any one garden area a five-year strawberry rotation. Strawberry diseases tend to live in the soil.

For best results, strawberries should be planted before you are really ready to be out in the garden. Like mid-April, when the ground is barely thawed and muddy, the raw wind is whistling and your hands are in imminent danger of frostbite.

Strawberries require good drainage and are really picky about the depth at which they are planted. You must put the baby plants in with the crowns just above the surface. If you cover the crown, the plant will die. If any roots are exposed, the plant may live, but it will not thrive.

Our experience with strawberries has been extensive enough to offer the following recommendations:

• *A two-year cycle*
• *Day-neutral varieties*
• *Raised planting beds for bigger, more-luscious berries*
• *Covering baby plants for the first week to protect the roots from becoming dry until they have a chance to get started.*

 I'm going to try the floating row covers you have recommended, but I don't want to haul back the rocks I have removed from the garden in order to hold the row covers down.

Isn't there a neater way to secure them?

 There is a very neat and easy answer — staples. Not the ones you keep in your desk drawer, of course, but big ones you make yourself from wire you probably have around the house. A wire coat hanger provides enough for two staples. The wire need not be that heavy, but it does have to be stiff enough to poke several inches into the ground. Choose wire that will not rust.

The staple needs to be an inch wide across the tip and have legs about six inches long — shorter if you have rocky soil. You do not poke the wire through the cover. Instead, make an ear of the fabric and put that under the little wicket, then shove the wire down flush with the ground. If you are using a relatively small cover, a staple at each corner will hold it. For large pieces, tack it down every 8 feet or so.

Row covers are great for germinating seeds, keeping them warm and moist. They are especially nice for small seeds. Once you germinate your carrots under a floating row cover, you will be a believer.

Will the row covers you advocate help keep bugs off my vegetables?

 About the only pests of this area that row covers will control are cabbage worms and root maggots. This is because the moths or flies fly in and lay their eggs, and the damage is done by the larvae. They are, however, very effective for those two problems. You needn't seal up every little hole to effectively exclude the moths.

Cabbage worms enjoy feasting on all the plants of the family, including broccoli, cauliflower, brussels sprouts and kale. Root maggots primarily attack radishes and onions, but also may go for the roots of very late plantings of the cabbage family.

 How in the Sam Hill do you plant onion plants? Sets are easy, but when I dig a trench and put the plants in, most of them fall over or grow up sideways. There must be a better way.

There is. It is an old English tool called a dibble or dibbler. About 9 inches long, it is rounded on top to fit in the palm of your hand. The bottom end tapers to a point. You simply poke it into the ground to whatever depth you choose and pull it out, leaving a hole about an inch in diameter.

Pop the onion plant into the hole deeper than you want it, pull it up to the correct height and the roots will be headed in the right direction. Then push dirt in to close the hole.

Don't bother asking for a dibble at your local store's garden department — we did, and most had never heard of them.

Being both inventive and frugal, we made our own dibbles from a short piece of broomstick, rounding off one end to hold, and sharpening the other to make holes. We have also found that a dandelion digger does a pretty good job.

I ordered some walls of water — when should I use them?

 A good rule of thumb is to put things out a month earlier than you would plan to do without the walls. Fill the tubes just full enough to make them stand up, but empty enough that the top folds almost together, making a tipi. (Later, when it's warmer and you want them open, you fill the tubes fuller and they stand up straighter.) Leave the water-filled tubes a few days so they have a chance to warm up the soil inside before you put in the plants or seeds.

We have put our broccoli and cabbage seedlings out in them very early. Cauliflower is pickier, and we recommend waiting a week after you put out cabbage and broccoli, setting out half your cauliflower plants and waiting another week — or even two — before putting out the rest. That way, at least some of them are pretty sure to survive.

For some reason, cauliflower is touchiest when it has six true leaves. If it gets too cold at that time, it does what is called "buttoning up," meaning it forms only little, teeny heads, about 2 inches in diameter.

About a month later, you can start putting out warm-season things like cucumbers, tomatoes, squash and melons. Although we start our tomatoes indoors, we find no advantage to putting cucumbers, squash or melons out as plants. We seed those directly in the walls of water. Besides, we note those crops don't like to have their roots disturbed by transplanting.

The reason behind planting in walls of water a month ahead of schedule is that, after a month, the plant will be too big to fit inside the wall. We know there are people who leave the walls on, sometimes for the entire season. But we see no reason to keep them on once the plant has grown out the top. We also see no reason to leave the plastic exposed to ultraviolet light all that time. They are not inexpensive and you don't want them to die any sooner than necessary.

Which brings us to another point: There seem to be a couple of sources whose walls are not of the best quality. We have had reports of some splitting in the first season. It could be inferior quality or maybe it has something to do with the conditions under which they were stored before sale, but if you have had some that split along the seams, we suggest you buy your replacements from a different source.

 Can I take the walls of water off my earlier plantings now and use them on the warm-weather seedlings?

 Juggling walls of water is a good idea. You might want to cover the plants you take them from if you expect frost for a while. The walls definitely should be removed when the plant is tall enough to come out the top or if it grows so big in there that it gets crowded.

When you take the walls off, empty and rinse them and put them somewhere protected to dry out. Stand them in the garage upside down or hang them from the clothesline to drain well, then set them right side up until they dry thoroughly.

Do not stand them on a cement driveway. One of us did that; the wind came up, stirred them around and wore holes in them. It is possible to mend leaks anywhere except on a seam. There is a 2-inch plastic tape which comes in clear and colors and which seals tears or holes if the surface is clean and dry when you apply it.

If you take care of them, walls of water will last several years. Some of ours are now six years old.

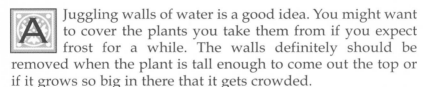 My tuberous begonias get so tall and gangly that they are ready to fall over by the time I want to put them outside. I start them in April in a south-southwest window where they get some afternoon sun. Any suggestions to get my begonias to grow more bushy and sturdy?

The plants' gangly growth suggests they may be getting too much heat for the amount of light they're receiving. Your note said you have a north window and we suggest you put them there. In any case, try to find them a cooler spot in the house which should help them to grow more slowly, and hence fuller.

If you keep them in the southern exposure, move them back 3 feet or so from the window where they still get good light but won't get so warm.

You are starting your tubers at the right time — late March or early April. You didn't say exactly how you do it, but we recommend starting each one in a 3-inch pot. Although some instructions say to set them at the surface, we find that covering the tubers with a half inch of dirt helps them develop a better root system.

When they are well up and the leaves are unfolding, it is time to move them to something bigger. They need a lot of depth — an 8- to 10-inch pot is about right.

Some begonias are just naturally taller than others. Perhaps yours are that sort. Almost all begonias need staking sooner or later, and staking them while they're still indoors is nothing to be ashamed of. If you put a stake in at the time of your last re-potting, you will avoid the hazard of stabbing the tuber later.

 The bagworms are back — isn't there any way to get rid of those disgusting little motating mudballs?

 The Bt (*Bacillus thuringiensis*) we have talked about for cabbage worms is the treatment of choice for bagworms, and if they are moving and feeding now, this is the moment to hit them.

You probably have no more than two weeks to deal with them. This "crawler" stage is the only time they are not protected by their thick mud shell. Spray with regular Bt, which is sold as Dipel, Thuricide and other trade names, and is widely available. Some dealers may not even know they have it, so you may want to look for it yourself.

They don't do a lot of harm—just leave little dead spots on the leaves wherever they stop for a meal. But it is rather revolting to pick yourself an arrangement of roses and find a dozen mud balls stuck to the back of a single leaf—or worse, to find a few lurking in the fresh dill you used to garnish your filet of sole.

Obnoxious as they may be, bagworms are rather interesting creatures. The name comes from the wingless female, which is technically a moth. She is an amorphous sack that lays the eggs and does nothing else. The eggs need no fertilization and some populations have no males at all.

The larvae protect themselves by building a shell with tiny grains of soil. The shape of this covering accounts for the creature's other name—the snailcase bagworm.

They are an imported pest which originated in Europe and, as far as we know, has no natural enemies here.

Georgianna dosed her bumper crop last year with Bt and this year has not found any live ones. With a fearless forefinger, she squashed any little mud huts she found in such sites as the underside of the bird bath and inside the eaves of the tool shed. She was elated when no yellow juice oozed out from any of the flattened worm homes.

We've had a couple of calls about bagworms; both gardeners are besieged by the crusty little critters. So evidently Georgianna's small crop really is due to her use of Bt last season. Another family also reported no bagworms after spraying with Bt the previous year.

A Montana native who fairly recently returned after liv-

Bt is a bacteria that kills only caterpillars and does not hurt anything else—not you or your cat or dog or the birds or bees or beneficial insects. Bagworms overwinter as partially developed larvae in protected areas like the bases of trees or around foundations. You need to spray for them after they emerge in the spring, but before they pupate.

ing out of the country for years says she never saw a bagworm here before she left, and when she came back they were rampant.

That jibes with our information that they immigrated from Europe fairly recently. They seem to like dry, shady places — like your mailbox, crevices in your board fence, the underside of leaves and the inside of cracks.

When one family lost a large limb from an old apple tree in a windstorm, they discovered the branch must have been cracked earlier, because the broken surfaces were encrusted with bagworms.

 At least two catalogs have a "mosquito plant" advertised as a "mosquito repellent that truly works." Do you know if it really does work?

 We saw articles in some gardening magazines about "citrosa," a plant allegedly developed by a Dutch scientist Dirk Van Leenen. Griffith Greenhouses, suppliers of citrosa, claimed that Van Leenen had created the plant by doing a gene transplant from lemon grass to a scented geranium.

Ads recommended one plant every 10 square feet around a patio as a mosquito barrier. At the price of $19.95 for two plants, it could be pretty expensive to surround a patio of any size.

"Avant Gardener" magazine later reported that after two years of searching, scientists at the University of Guelph in Ontario had been unable to find out anything about Van Leenen. In fact, their reports cast doubt on the very existence of citrosa as a new plant, saying that the gene transfers that were supposed to have been done are impossible with current technology.

Field tests by the Canadian researchers showed the plant to be ineffective as a mosquito repellent. Their lab tests showed it to be 30 to 40 percent effective if the leaves were crushed and rubbed on the skin, but the protection lasted only 30 minutes.

TOMATO VARIETIES

New last season was the currant tomato, the itsy-bitsy kind that comes in red and yellow and is touted for hanging pots. We have seen it listed in two catalogs as an heirloom variety. It's not. It's a wild variety native to Central America and northern South America.

Basically, all tomatoes except these are of the same species — *Lycopersicum esculentum*. (Occasionally it appears as *Lycopersicon esculentum* or *Lycopersicon lycopersicum*. Taxonomists are always renaming something. That's what *they* do in the winter.)

The currant tomato is *Lycopersicum pimpinellifolium*. As far as we can determine, there has been no breeding of cultivars.

We tried some currant tomatoes last year. We found them to be rangier than the "Red Robin" cherry tomatoes we prefer. They have more stem, much smaller leaves and more empty spaces between. They were early enough to produce tomatoes even in a really terrible tomato year and they did have good flavor. But they also had tough skins.

They were interesting to try because they are different, but not something we think many gardeners are likely to adopt as a favorite.

We have had an interesting experience with the aforementioned "Red Robin" tomatoes we have grown for years in 6-inch pots in a sunny window or in the greenhouse. For the first four years, the seed came from one source, but last year we bought it elsewhere. One cannot tell where any of the seed was actually grown, but obviously the two sources offer different strains of the same variety.

With the first ones, we got one good crop when the plant reached about 2 feet tall, although it was still growing. Then it sickened or acquired bugs and got composted.

The seeds from the new source never grew over 15 inches. When it first grew, the foliage was so dense you had to get in there and prune some out to provide air circulation and to prevent molds. When we got the first crop, the plant was still grow-ing, but it got a little more sprawly and we got another crop.

All this proves is that plants aren't all clones of each other, which makes it more fun—the eternal learning experi-ence of gardening.

 I have several Miss Kim dwarf lilacs and one of them has grown larger than any of the others, but has not bloomed in the three years it has lived with me. What could be its problem?

There are several possibilities. One is that if it has put on more growth, it has been pouring all its energies into leaves and growth and it may get around to blooming later.

There also could be something wrong with that particu-lar bush. Digging in a little high-phosphorus fertilizer might help, but of course, not until next year.

It is possible that the bush is not what you thought it was—there is always a chance of mislabeling. Or, it could just be a peculiar plant and not typical of the species.

If you really want a lilac in that spot, we'd recommend digging this one up and replacing it. If it's a nice-looking bush and you don't care about a couple weeks of blooms, you may de-cide to leave it to do its thing. Or if you are tolerant and patient, you can wait a year or two and see if your bush will eventually bloom. (For reasons as yet unknown, this bush did bloom a lot in its fourth season.)

Summer

CONTINUED NEXT PAGE

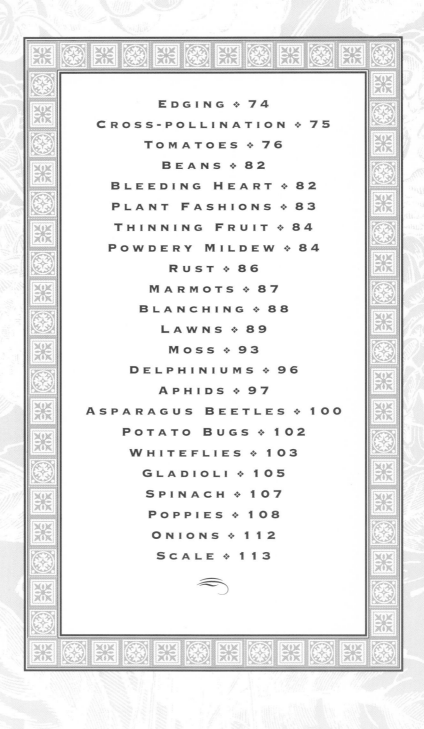

My peonies are spindly and don't bloom well. Is it possible I have planted them too deep?

 It is possible, but it is more likely that they would not bloom at all if they were planted too deep. Depth is critical to peonies. You don't want the buds on the surface, but you also don't want more than 2 inches of soil over the little pink nubbins that are the flower buds.

If you think they are too deep, you can check by sticking your finger down in the moist soil to see if you can touch a bud.

A late frost can kill the bloom buds, too. Although some peonies are hardy to 40 degrees below zero, many are better-suited to a climate like Seattle's. May and June are the usual bloom times for peonies in this area, but if you have an earlier variety, it may never bloom well because more years than not the buds will get killed.

There is no guarantee that plants are acclimated to this area just because you buy them locally. Our capricious warm-up/cool-down weather can get them if it happens at the wrong time for the buds.

Peonies need full or nearly full sun and won't bloom well without it. They do not tolerate root competition, so should not be planted where tree roots or grass impinge on their territory.

It takes a plant about three years to get established and a year for any flower buds to form, so if you have a 4-year-old peony that has only two blooms on it, don't give up yet.

Once established, however, peonies are one of the longest-lived flowers in the garden. It is not unusual for a plant to live 50 years. Therefore, it pays to give it some special care.

Peonies appreciate a little phosphate boost at planting time and an annual dose of all-purpose fertilizer thereafter. Plant your roots in good soil—if it's not good, work in organic material. They prefer an acid-neutral soil—pH 6 or 7. Peony roots are fairly brittle, so firm the soil around them gently, but don't tamp down too hard. They like more water than we get naturally, so plan to give them a little extra.

Diseases that affect peonies are mostly fungal and rare in this climate. Not many bugs like peonies. The ants that usually visit the flower buds are totally harmless. They like the sweet sticky stuff on the bud scales. They don't hurt the peony and they are not necessary for the buds to open.

Nobody knows what the original peonies were like because they have been bred for many hundreds of years. They probably originated in the Orient — they appear in very old Oriental art and as cultivated, rather than wild, flowers. There are not a lot of new cultivars being developed now because there are so many good old ones.

Peonies come in single, semi-double and double forms in colors ranging from white through the pinks to dark maroon. There are not many of the Chinese and Japanese single varieties that are hardy in this area.

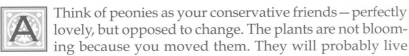

 My peonies were always lovely but they were in a bad spot, so last fall I moved them. Now the plants look fine but they are not blooming. What did I do wrong?

Think of peonies as your conservative friends — perfectly lovely, but opposed to change. The plants are not blooming because you moved them. They will probably live longer than you do and will return to normal, but first they have to sulk a little while. Some may bloom next year and some may take three or four years.

Different peonies are different. If your neighbor says she moved hers the same time you did and hers are all blooming, don't assume she did something better than you did. Just because it takes one plant a long time to get itself organized does not mean it hasn't virtues in other areas.

Just make sure that your peonies are getting enough sun in their new location and that they aren't being crowded by grass — peonies resent grass.

Did you replant the crowns at the right depth? The bud eyes should be no more than 2 inches under the surface. If you buried them too deep, don't dig them up and raise them—remove dirt from the top and leave them in a depression. And if you go prospecting around there, do it very carefully to protect the brittle roots and buds.

 I was given a geranium two years ago. It bloomed outdoors all summer and inside all winter, but when I set it out last year, it stopped blooming and the leaves turned red. How can I keep that from happening when I put it out this summer?

The leaves' turning red is almost surely due to the sudden doses of high light. Even if it had been in a window with sun all day and then was taken outdoors to where it gets sun only part of the day, it could be getting up to 100 times as much light as it was receiving inside.

It probably quit blooming because it was having a hard time—it's the first thing a plant can do when it is stressed. It then devotes all its energy to coping with the stress.

You need to get it used to the light levels before leaving it outside. Take it out to a spot in the deep shade and bring it in at night for at least three days. Then let it have only a little morning sun for a few days. If nights are warm consistently, you can start leaving it out.

Don't change its location more than every three or four days. By early June, it should be adjusted and ready for its summer home.

Why did the cucumber and squash plants I started in the house turn white when I set them out?

 They were probably not acclimated to the massive increase in light. They may survive, but they could just burn up—the leaves turn dry and brown and fall off. When setting out plants, remember that they need time to adjust to the vastly different conditions under which they will be living. Set your babies out in a protected spot, out of the wind and where they will be in the shade at least from noon on. Leave them for a couple of days before moving them to a somewhat sunnier spot for a day or two and before planting in the garden. They will be adapting to temperature as well as to light.

In the house, the plants have not been stressed. When they are put outdoors, their epidermal coverings have to toughen and thicken. It is quite amazing how fast young plants do this.

 My baby broccoli plants have holes in the leaves. Some are so bad I'm afraid they are going to disappear altogether. What's doing that and what can I do about it?

 Flea beetles are almost certainly the perpetrators. They love the cole family more than anything else and they specialize in eating the babies. They don't seem to find the plants nearly as delicious once the leaves reach about 3 inches in length.

Flea beetles are little tiny black things that hop just like fleas do—a very long distance, too, for such a small creature.

They are extremely fast and their calling card is lots of teeny holes in leaves. To look at one, you wouldn't think he could do much damage, but when a bunch of hungry ones get together for lunch, they can pretty much finish off a young plant.

The ideal solution is prevention. Next year, start your

broccoli in the house five or six weeks ahead of the date you want to set them out.

If it's already too late for that this year, your second-best bet is to put on floating row covers until the plants achieve sufficient size. Won't you trap the little beetles under the cover? You will find they hop away when you just come near a plant with your hand, so brush the plants gently and pop the covers on quickly.

Plan C is to dust the plants with talcum or baby powder, which is reasonably helpful. Perhaps the bugs don't like the smell. It also has the advantage of making you feel that you are doing something for the problem.

 Can you tell me some scab-resistant potato varieties?

 Among white potatoes (which, of course, are really brown) Frontier Russet, Russet Burbank, Butte and Onaway are particularly resistant to scab. Caribe, a purple-skinned potato with white meat, also resists the disease. For red varieties, you might try Norland or Red Dale.

In deciding whether to plant red or white, remember that red potatoes have a waxy consistency and so don't mash or bake well. They're great for potato salad because they don't fall apart when boiled. They tend to be a little earlier but generally don't keep all winter.

White potatoes' mealy texture makes them best for baking and mashing, but they are more apt to turn to mush when boiled. They are the better keepers.

This is an excellent potato-growing area, but conditions that make potatoes do well also are the ones in which scab flourishes. It's not hard to see why it is called scab—the spots look like the dried scabs on a little boy's knees after a bike wreck. Scab is harmless and only skin deep—it's just ugly.

If you grew scabby potatoes last year, plant them someplace else this season. The organisms that cause scab stay in the soil for many years. Scab often is carried in manure, which is one way you can get it in a place you never had it before.

Some people dust seed potatoes with sulfur in an effort to prevent scab, but we are not convinced it has that effect. The practice probably came from the fact that sulfur is used to make soil more acid, a condition scab does not appreciate.

 Last year many of my potatoes had little black spots under the skin. What causes that and what can I do to prevent it this year?

 We don't know what the black dots are. Potatoes are subject to lots of diseases that, because they turn up so seldom, are of interest only to commercial growers. Many of these maladies appear because of specific weather conditions and you won't see them again until exactly the same set of circumstances recur. One thing you don't have to worry about is late blight, a real curse and the cause of the Irish potato famine. The plants just die late in the season and there's nothing to do for it. Fortunately, we don't have late blight here.

There are potato hazards you can do something about. One preventable situation is rotting potato sets. For some reason, potatoes grow better when you plant pieces of large potatoes instead of whole small ones. The ideal size is a 1-inch cube. A cube shape seems to produce better results than a wedge.

Potatoes need fertilizer, but too much nitrogen results in glorious tops and a smaller number of tubers. It also appears that planting a chunk with too many eyes results in fewer tubers. One eye is enough, two or three are OK, but discard the portion of the potato with a cluster of eyes.

Be sure you start with certified seed potatoes. Many diseases are carried in seed potatoes, and viruses are especially hard to get rid of once they are introduced to your garden. Certified seed potatoes are inspected and guaranteed free of any common diseases.

If you want to use your own last year's potatoes for seed you can, but if you keep doing that year after year, you are asking for trouble. Try trading your last season's potatoes for your neighbor's.

Potatoes you buy at the grocery store for food probably have been treated to prevent them from sprouting. Even if they grow, they are likely not to be as healthy as those grown from good seed potatoes.

Commercial growers often cut up their seed potatoes weeks ahead of time and allow them to develop a dry "skin" over the cut surfaces. This is called "suberizing" and it requires careful control of temperature, humidity and oxygen level.

Conditions here are usually just about right to suberize your seed potatoes if you just cut them up and plant them in the ground. It doesn't hurt to let the pieces dry, so if you have been doing this and having good crops, keep on doing it. If you haven't, don't bother.

You can read all sorts of pronouncements on planting depth and spacing, all disagreeing with each other. Don't pay any attention to directions that say to plant potatoes 10 inches apart. Potatoes here are very likely to grow 50 to 100 percent larger than in other parts of the country.

Plant your seed at least 2 inches deep—3 or 4 inches is probably better. Not planting deep enough is one factor that can reduce the yield.

A couple of potatoes' favorite things about the area are our cool nights and cool soil temperature. Once a potato plant has enough leaves, it begins making tubers. It slows down considerably when soil temperature reaches 68 degrees and stops entirely if it gets to 84 degrees. Our soil never gets that hot and only gets to 68 in a really hot spell.

If you want to start your potatoes early and are afraid they will freeze, just pile dirt on the plants when a cold snap is expected. They will find it far easier to come up through the added dirt than to recover from having their tops frozen.

While we're on the subject of piling on dirt, you will eventually want to hill up your potato plants to keep the tubers cool and out of the sunlight. You can either do this automatically when the plants reach a height of 6-8 inches or just keep an eye on them and do it when the tubers are close to the surface.

If potatoes are exposed to light while growing or in storage, they develop alkaloids that turn their color green and their flavor bitter.

 A neighborly gopher has nibbled all the blossoms off my potato plants. Will they still make potatoes?

 Not to worry. All the blossoms do is indicate when a plant has potatoes big enough to eat. Some potatoes don't even bloom at all.

 Some of my potato plants made fruits that look like little green tomatoes. Will they ripen? If they do, can I grow potatoes from their seeds?

 In theory you can, indeed, grow potatoes from the seeds these fruits produce. We don't know what a ripe potato seed looks like—neither of us has ever seen a mature one.

People who publish on potatoes agree that you will get a better crop by planting seed potatoes, rather than potato seeds. (Word order can make a big difference, can't it?)

It might be fun to try ripening and planting your seeds just to see what happens. You might enjoy the challenge of growing some to cross-pollinate and produce your own hybrid. We wouldn't recommend, however, that you depend on the seeds for your main crop.

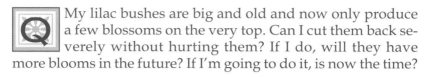

My lilac bushes are big and old and now only produce a few blossoms on the very top. Can I cut them back severely without hurting them? If I do, will they have more blooms in the future? If I'm going to do it, is now the time?

Yes, yes and yes. Soon after blossoming finishes is the time to prune spring-blooming shrubs such as lilacs, and pruning will help your old bushes start flowering again. There are three levels of severity you could employ.

The least radical is to remove about a fifth of the old wood at ground level, including the tallest stem. If your bush has 10 major stems, cut off two of them. Then cut off at the ground most of the suckers around the bush, leaving five or six to provide new growth.

This is the way bushes that are not overgrown should be pruned every year. If you do, you will allow some of the babies to mature and get rid of some of the old wood. The best blooms are not on the oldest wood.

You don't need to cut off old blossoms—it won't affect next year's bloom. So if you do cut them off, it can be just because you are sick of looking at the dried-up brown things.

The most drastic way to deal with an overgrown bush is to cut it all back to a height of 18 inches. Cut off all but five or six suckers. Do not cut the old growth any shorter than 18 inches until you have some new stuff coming up—your lilac may have been grafted to rootstock of another species and you wouldn't have the same lilac any more.

If you follow this path, your bush will not bloom next year, but you will be rid of all the old wood; the lilac doesn't mind the operation.

A middle-of-the-road approach is to cut out about half the old wood at ground level and next year cut the other half. That way you get some bloom next year.

Once you have done this major pruning, you can shape your bush. Stand back and look at it. Cut out anything that's ugly. Open it up for better air circulation if it's too dense. Trim it to your desired size.

The same basic methods can be applied to any spring-blooming shrub, although not all can stand to be cut back as drastically as lilacs. You can cut out one of every five main stems, remove suckers and thin.

If you have to prune a shrub severely every year because it gets too big, it's probably in the wrong spot. Take it out and replace it with something smaller—the nurseryman or catalog will tell you what size the plant will attain.

Note for Beginning Bulb Gardeners

When your tulips and daffodils are finishing up, cut off the faded blooms and stems if you like, but leave the foliage, even when it starts looking brown and ugly. Weigh it down with a few small stones, if you want, to keep it out of the way once it's no longer green.

Plant a bunch of annuals among your bulbs to hide the old leaves, but don't remove them. It is through those leaves that the bulbs gather the energy to make next year's blossom buds. Remember, don't plant perennials with your bulbs—the roots and bulbs live on the same level and as they multiply, crowd each other out.

I have lost several lettuce plants lopped off at ground level. I assume cutworms did it — what can I do?

 Cutworms live in the top few inches of the soil. There are several species, all of which are the larvae of ordinary moths. Some eat just above the ground and some just under the surface.

They are a late spring and early summer problem, which means they are most numerous when plants are young and tender and the worms can eat them whole or do sufficient damage to kill them.

Prevention is the best defense. When you find a plant a cutworm has attacked, start looking for the worm. If you check daily and search immediately, you won't have to look very far — it will probably be in the top inch of soil and not more than 3 or 4 inches from its victim.

If you lose four or five lettuce plants in a row in one night, you don't have a lot of cutworms. It's probably just one. Find it and kill it. You don't want to spray for cutworms because to kill them you have to use something so strong it will kill your earthworms. If you can't bring yourself to search and destroy, there are protections you can provide your plants.

You can put a large nail or a wooden farmer match on each side of the plant right next to the stem to prevent the worm from curling around the stem and getting a good bite.

You can make 2-inch collars of newspaper or foil and wrap them around the stem an inch above the ground and an inch below, but be careful you don't break the plant off in the process. You can also put a section of milk carton or a can around the plant, making sure it extends from an inch above to an inch below ground level.

I haven't any perennials yet, but would like to get some started. How can I decide which plants to buy?

Nothing is sure-fire. What works for your neighbor may not work for you. However, start by choosing only things hardy to Zone 4. If you have a nice sheltered microclimate or you feel particularly brave, you can plant some things hardy only to Zone 5.

Look at bloom time as well. Things that say they bloom in the fall often freeze here before they have a chance to flower; this has proved to be the case with some asters and chrysanthemums.

Choose things that say they like neutral or alkaline soil, not acid. Azaleas and hydrangeas like acid soil and are also very delicate for our climate. If you really want them, save them for a few years down the road, when you are an old hand at perennial-farming.

Even observing the above cautions, you still have thousands of perennial plants you can grow here. There are so many that you won't have time to try them all.

Since you have never grown perennials, it would be best to start with things you have seen and liked, or at least heard of. Later, as your experience and confidence grow, you may want to branch out into some things you have not seen here. If your catalog or label says your favorite plant is hardy to Zone 7, you will have to move to grow it successfully.

Start by assessing your space. Ask yourself, "Is my planting area big enough for this plant when it's full-grown?" and "Do I want something 6 feet tall, or something that reaches only 8 inches?"

Consider the light in your planting area. Almost all annuals need full sun, but perennials come in a whole range of light tolerances, from deep shade to full sun. Most need good drainage.

Take maintenance into consideration. Some perennials

require only your admiration, but others must have their seed-pods removed every other day. Peonies are practically carefree, but columbine has to be deadheaded to keep it blooming.

If you have very many plants that need deadheading, it gets to be time-intensive. But if you have that extra time, they will reward you with long and colorful blooming seasons.

Another thing to find out before buying a perennial is how often it will need dividing. Most need to be separated after about four years, but some more often. Does the plant self-sow? Some never multiply, but some scatter about with great abandon.

Our best advice boils down to learning as much as you can about the habits of any perennial you are considering and starting with a few you really admire and know you have the time and inclination to care for.

If anything shows signs of conquering your horticultural world, dig out all signs of it and plant a bit in a pot. Put it on the patio, or bury it in the flower bed, leaving an inch or so of pot rim above soil level to contain it.

If some of your first perennials keel over and refuse all attempts at resuscitation, do not consider yourself a failure as a gardener. The same thing goes for any setbacks you suffer in the garden. Those things happen to all of us.

The two of us have a combined total years of gardening experience so high we can't calculate them (nor do we want to), yet we have seeds that refuse to germinate, perennials that won't repeat, crops that don't amount to the cost of the seed and bugs that thumb their tiny noses at us.

When we have a failure we feel stupid, then sad, then mad and then determined. We may be determined never to plant that thing again, or we may be determined to keep trying until we get it right. Gardening is not an exact science, but it's satisfying, it's healthy and it gives you something to talk about at church circle or Rotary.

What is the easiest way to keep the grass out of my flower bed?

 There is no easy way — only hard and harder. Over the years, we have tried just about anything anybody suggested. Trials with "easy" ways leave one very disillusioned.

Installing edging material — metal, plastic, wood, brick, etc. — will slow down the takeover by fine, long grasses, but quack grass is not deterred for even one minute by edging. Quack grass has been known to dive 36 inches to get under a barrier.

Landscape cloth can be useful, but only for a year or two. If you leave it down longer, it makes an industrial-strength mess. Grass and weeds do grow down through it and come up through it, no matter what the ads and salesmen say.

Georgianna is having a major headache with hers because her landscaper put the cloth down before seeding the lawn. The grass — and dandelions — seem to prefer growing down through the bark and black cloth to living in the topsoil-covered rocks of the lawn.

Landscape cloth is a fine way to get a new plant, shrub or tree established. Dig out all the grass and weeds around the newcomer and cover the area with something opaque. Leave it for one season and then take it out of there. Besides the problems already mentioned, leaving the material down also prevents your plant from spreading and putting up new stems.

If you don't mind the looks of dead grass, you can spray a strip along the bed with an herbicide. You will have a tan strip edging your bed for the first half of the summer, but in the second half the grass will be back. You also must be extremely careful not to let any herbicide drift onto your garden plants or they will die, too. And they won't be back later in the summer.

In the long run, the most effective and least arduous method we have found is to simply cut around the bed with an edger and remove the grass and roots by hand. We have never used power edgers, but there are several types—some attached to tillers.

Hand edging is not hard if you don't have a lot of rocks. Just go around everything once in a season, taking off at least an inch of the grass. Molly calls it "painless enlargement." Gardeners know that the larger the beds and the smaller the lawn, the less work you have.

The English edge this way, but leave a little ditch so the grass roots have to grow deeper to jump from lawn to bed.

Get yourself a good-ish edger and keep it sharp. Sharpen it after only a couple of sessions of edging—not just every couple years. Make a few cuts immediately after sharpening the blade and you will see the difference it makes. If you have to jump on your edger, it's dull and you are working too hard.

If you are looking for a miracle method, we don't know one. Anything advertised as a miracle method is just going to be expensive and will probably only last one season.

 What about that old gardeners' wives' tale that says you must keep squash, cucumbers and tomatoes separate in the garden? Is that necessary?

 Unless you plan to save seed from one or more of the crops, it is completely unnecessary—as long as you can keep the squash plants from strangling the tomatoes. Tomatoes are not a cross-pollination problem, but any of the plants called cucurbits—melons, cucumbers, squash, gourds and pumpkins—will cross-breed. So if you grow a squash you just love and want to save its seeds, you must first be sure that it is not a hybrid variety. Even if it is not (non-hybrids are identified as open-pollinated or heirloom varieties) you still have to see that no pollen from any other variety reaches the plant.

This means that either it must be far enough from any other cucurbit that a bee can't carry pollen from one kind to the other, or you must grow it under cover of cheesecloth or other row cover and pollinate it yourself with a Q-Tip or paintbrush.

If you have a squash whose flavor you adore but whose color offends you, and you decide to cross it, be prepared for a long process. For every good cross there are 1,000 bad ones.

 How do I get the most out of my little home garden tomato patch?

 Here you are — all the tricks we can think of to produce tomatoes that are the earliest, biggest and most productive. You won't be able to do all three things from one variety, but with different plants, you can have some of each.

Tomatoes are native to Central and South America, where they are tender perennials. Montana's climate does not treat them kindly. Just keep in mind that you are trying to convince your tomato plants that they are living in Kentucky instead of Montana.

To get tomatoes early, you must start with early varieties. Look for ones bred to set fruit with night temperatures as low as 40 degrees. If temperatures are above 95 or below 55, many tomatoes will not set fruit.

To start your tomatoes from seed, begin early — at least six, but not more than eight weeks ahead of the date you plan to set them out. This will be five minutes after the last frost. In an unprotected place, it will be about June 1. If you live right in town or in another protected area, it can be as early as mid-May.

It is important to keep your seedlings growing steadily, which requires that they be re-potted twice, or perhaps even more. Transplant babies from their six-packs into a 2-inch pot, and from there to a 4-inch container, etc. Do not put the little ones directly into a big pot, thinking you will save some time. You will be writing an invitation to root rot fungi.

Each time you re-pot, set the plant down past its lower leaf. Tomatoes grow roots from their stems, and deep-setting helps them establish a good root system.

Walls of water allow you to set out tomatoes a month earlier than you otherwise could. If you are going to put your tomatoes in walls of water, count back an extra month before last frost date to start your seeds. Don't plan to leave the walls of water on longer than a month, because the plant gets too tall and the top might freeze.

Pick a place to plant tomatoes where there is shelter — in front of a south wall is ideal, especially if it's brick or stone, which re-radiate the sun's heat.

Plastic spread over the planting area for a week before transplanting will warm the soil. You may use black or clear plastic, although weeds will grow under clear sheets and not under black. You can leave the plastic down as mulch after you plant, to keep the soil warm, but remember you have to get water to the plants.

When you plant a tomato in the ground, plant it sideways in a shallow trench, carefully bending the top up above soil level to avoid snapping the brittle stems. This puts the roots in the warmest part of the soil.

Giving transplants a drink of half-strength liquid fertilizer helps reduce transplant shock. Recent tests have shown that an epsom salt solution at transplant time increases yield.

Unless it is extremely well-protected, build your tomato a windbreak. You can make it a clear plastic cage, open on the top, by making a square or circle of sticks and stretching plastic around it. It's a good idea to give tomatoes a little fertilizer once a month throughout the growing season, but do not use manure or other high-nitrogen fertilizers or you will wind up with lots of leaves and not many tomatoes.

For the biggest crop, although not quite as early and with somewhat smaller fruits, cage your tomatoes. You can't believe the size estimates on your seed packets because our long summer days make the plants grow bigger. You need a cage taller than those commonly sold in garden departments. Get fencing 3 to 4 feet wide and bend it into cages 12-18 inches in diameter.

Prune off the stuff that grows outside the cage. This gives the plant light and air and makes it easy to get at.

To get the earliest and largest tomatoes, although in lower numbers, prune and stake your plants. When you transplant to the garden, leave one, or at most two stems, and cut off the others.

Set a 5-foot stake on the west or northwest side of the plant (because that's where our prevailing winds come from) and tie the plant to it at 1-foot intervals. Use anything soft, like green cotton yarn or fabric strips, or recycle snaggy old nylons. Cross the material between plant and stake, forming a figure eight. This prevents the tie from becoming too tight as the stem grows thicker and also helps prevent wind damage.

As the plant grows, keep cutting off side branches that develop, leaving the first leaf to provide shade for fruit and the leaf surface necessary for the plant to produce fruit. When the plant reaches the top of the stake, start cutting off the top.

The most tomatoes per square foot of garden area (but not the most per plant) may be achieved by planting them as close as 1 foot apart, but under those conditions, plants must be pruned and staked.

WARNING: Before you prune a tomato plant, be positive it is the indeterminate type, which keeps on growing. If you start amputating parts of a determinate—or bush-type—plant, you will be cutting off the fruiting parts and will wind up with a lovely, shapely green plant, but no tomatoes.

Come August 1, cut off all blossoms. The plant will keep right on making them, but just continue clipping them off. There is no way you will get fruit from a blossom that comes on that late. Removing the blossoms, however, makes a significant difference in the size and ripeness of the fruits the plant has already set.

If you are unwilling to cage, stake or prune, you can just let your plants sprawl. Our ground is usually dry enough to prevent the fruit from rotting. However, be prepared for them to claim an inordinate share of the garden area or to sneak around under the zucchini where it's dark and the tomatoes won't ripen.

A recently published study from Michigan State University recommends fertilizing tomatoes with low quantities of nitrogen and phosphates to promote sturdy, compact plants. Then three to five days before transplanting to the garden, give the seedlings a good shot of all-purpose fertilizer. It takes the plants about five days to take up the nutrients and eight days to start putting out new shoots to give them a big growth spurt after transplant.

Be sure when setting out your plants that they don't have any baby tomatoes on them. If they have some, remove them. Otherwise, your crop will be 10 days later. In plants with fruit, the nutrients needed to develop the plant go to the fruit instead. Researchers tracked carbohydrate use in tomato plants and found that to be what made the difference. Setting out plants with buds and blossoms does not seem to have the same effect.

 None of my tomatoes are doing anything. Even my Early Girls are just sitting there. What can I do?

 Variety is tremendously important in how tomatoes do when we have a cold, cloudy summer. Oregon Spring is one of the few varieties that will continue to look happy. Such a year is not one to grow tomatoes that would thrive in New Jersey. It is a year to say, "This may not be a year for tomatoes, but I've never had such cauliflower before." And you might want to add, "I don't care if I never see another raspberry."

The Early Girls will not be anywhere near as happy with cool weather as those bred by James Baggett at Oregon State University for the cool, cloudy weather west of the Cascades.

Molly's mom noted that it is easy to tell the optimist gardener from the pessimist gardener in a cold summer. The optimist talks about the glorious peas, lettuce and cauliflower;

the pessimist is the one talking about the sad cucumbers, melons and short corn.

But don't despair when the weather is unkind. And don't forget to murmur a few motivational phrases as you weed and fertilize.

 My tomatoes bloomed like mad, but they aren't making any tomatoes. Why? Was it because it was too cold or wet for the bees to pollinate them?

 No. Tomatoes are self-pollinating. They have a complete flower with both pistil and pollen, arranged so the movement of the flowers dumps pollen on the pistil, fertilizing it. That's why you can grow cherry tomatoes on your sunny windowsill inside.

If you have plants in the squash family — squash, cucumbers and melons — that are not producing, absence of bees may be the cause. They require cross-pollination.

The problem with your tomatoes is more likely that they are just very late. They may still be coming, even if it's not a great year for tomatoes. As long as we don't have an early frost, you may get more than you think.

Also, as we have mentioned before, variety is very important in weird weather years. Varieties you have grown with great success in years past may be a complete bust in a cold summer. Some varieties are just not programmed for cold and damp.

The ones bred for Siberia and the Canadian prairies, such as the cultivars of Manitoba's sub-Arctic, are unlikely to do well because, while they like cold nights, cool days are just not for them.

The tomatoes likely to do the best in a cool year are those bred for the northern Pacific Coast — San Francisco north.

Of course, you may not get tomatoes at all. Nothing will make some tomatoes set fruit in difficult weather conditions. They may just bloom and then go back to sleep, saying, "It's too cold. I don't want to have babies this year, thank you."

Last year I tried growing tomatoes in containers. They grew into beautiful plants, but they never set fruit. What did I do wrong?

 The cause of the problem is probably not you but the variety of tomato you planted. Don't give up. Just be sure when you plant this year's crop you use only a variety the catalog or seed envelope says is suitable for containers.

Too small a container could also prevent fruiting, but the five-gallon containers you used should be plenty big for any tomato plant. Many small tomatoes don't need anywhere near that much space.

Try a determinate, small plant this time. Determinate plants grow to a specific height and stop. You do not prune them because they fruit on their side stems.

Our season with its very cold nights can be a problem, too. If the tomato variety is not good for cold temperatures, it may bloom well, but will not set fruit if night temperatures fall below 50 degrees.

You also need to be sure you are planting a short-season tomato. A variety requiring a long season may just be getting ready to bloom or to set fruit when our season is over. Check the number of days to maturity and choose a very short one, or start your seeds very early indoors and haul the container outside and back in as the weather dictates.

Most container-friendly types are small-fruited. Our personal favorite is Red Robin because of its delicious flavor and thin skin. Its plant size is perfect for a 6-inch pot. Molly grows them all winter on her windowsill.

Cool roots are extremely important to tomatoes, and container plants take special care. Either insulate the pots well by wrapping them with something or shade them during the hot part of the day.

Some of my green beans are weird. They are funny little stubs with no leaves on them. What did I do?

 These plants are called "blind" and the condition comes from damaged seeds. The injury could have occurred at harvest or afterward in storage, but probably happened before you ever got them. It is very easy to hurt bean seeds.

The blind plants will probably just stay that way and never sprout any leaves, so you might as well pull them out.

 Why have my bleeding hearts stopped blooming? My neighbor's are still at it and she says they bloom all summer long.

These must be two different types of bleeding hearts. The old-fashioned kind, which yours must be, blooms during May and June and then, no matter what you do, will not bloom again until next spring.

This is *Dicentra spectabilis*. This is the largest bleeding heart. A native of the Orient, it was taken to England in 1847.

Your neighbor probably had a fern-leafed variety, which blooms all season. *Eximia* is native to the eastern United States. Its name means "distinguished." *Formosa*, meaning "beautiful," is native to the western United States. These have begun appearing in catalogs only fairly recently.

All garden plants, of course, came originally from the wild. *Dicentra spectabilis* was a wild flower in China and Japan. We have some wild versions of *Dicentra* here—Dutchman's breeches and steershead.

The craze for cultivating foreign wild flowers had its first real boom in Holland in the 1600s when the first tulip bulbs started arriving from Turkey, where they grew all over the hillsides. During "tulipomania," special bulbs were acquired for the equivalent of $500 to $1,000.

But as suddenly as the business started, it was over. The Dutch nurserymen learned to breed tulips. Fortunes were lost by those who had spent large sums on a bulb in the hope of selling the offset bulblets. All of a sudden, a $1,000 bulb was all but worthless.

The late 17th and early 18th century was an era of plant hunters, especially for the English, who were big gardeners and avid explorers. The two interests naturally combined. Expeditions were usually financed by some wealthy gardener and directed by a botanist. Some of the plants brought home already had been cultivated in Asia, but many did not become garden flowers until they got to Europe.

In the days of Washington and Jefferson, both great gardeners, it was the fashion to grow European plants instead of American natives. Some of the popular varieties were European and some had been obtained originally from Asia.

The Europeans, however, showed no interest in cultivating American native plants until their explorers began investigating our Northwest Coast. The climate there was compatible with England's and the plant hunters were particularly excited about some trees.

They did not, of course, establish forests of sequoia or Douglas fir in the English countryside, but they were eager to have a few garden specimens.

More recently — since World War II — there has been more interest in American native plants and the exchange goes on. Things bred in one place get taken somewhere else, cultivars develop and those are later taken back to the country of origin. In southern California, where water is ever more scarce, gardeners are currently eager to obtain the drought-resistant native plants of southern Africa and Australia.

I have never had apple trees before, but we have moved to a house with several in the yard. A neighbor says we need to thin the fruit. Is that true and if so, why?

 Your neighbor is giving you good advice. While thinning is not absolutely necessary, it will improve the quality of the crop and the health of the trees.
Once the trees have finished the "June drop," when marble-size apples fall, it's time to thin. June drop is the tree's way of dealing with a crop too big to be supported by the leaves the tree has. To get a small number of larger fruit and to reduce stress on the tree, you can go out and remove more little apples.

Hand thin your crop to leave fruit 4-6 inches apart. This applies to plums, apricots, peaches and pears, as well as apples. Do not thin cherries or crab apples.

We have read that the ideal situation is to have 40 leaves for each apple for the best-quality fruit. We have also read that the best is 35 leaves to the apple and 6-8 inches apart for the fruit. If you know anybody willing to come and count the leaves on your apple trees, please send him around!

Unless you thin your fruit, it is easy to get into an alternate-year bearing cycle. If you have too big a crop and do not thin, you will have no crop the following year.

 The leaves of my tuberous begonias are covered with powdery mildew. Is there a cure?

 Unfortunately, the answer for powdery mildew lies more with prevention than cure. Fungicide only works if you put it on before you have mildew. You could dust things all season and never get it, but you would never know if you would have had it without the fungicide.

Georgianna reports partial success because she had a "pilot plant" in her rose garden that was particularly susceptible to the disease. As soon as it showed up on that, she dusted all the other roses. It didn't help the pilot any, but may have saved many of the others.

Powdery mildew gets on lots of things. Some — like roses, greenhouse cucumbers and tomatoes — are seriously affected. Others — like lilacs and peas — can be covered with it and not mind a bit.

It is not much of a problem in dry conditions, so keeping plants thinned to promote air circulation may help. Ironically, another thing that may help is misting the plants because the spores need a dry surface to adhere to.

 Last year after my lilacs finished blooming, the leaves got covered with a white dust. What is it? Will it be back? Will it hurt the bush?

 The stuff is powdery mildew. It may be back, but it won't hurt the lilac. Whether or not it returns depends on weather conditions. Cool, wet weather after bloom promotes mildew. The tiny fungi put down root-like threads into the leaf, but the leaf remains healthy.

If the sight of it bothers you, there is something you can try — and powdery mildew does harm other plants. For instance, it will deform the stems and buds of roses.

A plant pathologist at Cornell University, Dr. R.K. Horst, studied the problem and came up with a spray for use on plants exhibiting powdery mildew.

His recipe calls for one tablespoon of baking soda and two or three teaspoons of Sunspray summer oil to a gallon of water.

Horst doesn't know if the oil participates in the extermination of the mildew or if it simply serves as a spreader-sticker. (Spreader-sticker is a semiofficial term for an oil mixed into a water-based spray to keep it where you put it. You can buy commercially produced spreader-stickers, too.)

Summer oils other than Sunspray would probably work

the same way, but it is the only brand licensed by the federal government for use on vegetables.

We stress that this is a purely experimental treatment and not registered with the Environmental Protection Agency. It is a violation of federal law to recommend it, but we can report that this man had good luck with it for powdery mildew and black spot on roses, phlox and zinnias and on foliar vegetable diseases.

You should also make sure your plants and bushes have good air circulation. Thin any thick, heavy bushes by pruning. We have naturally low humidity here, which is a plus.

Two master gardeners in Texas heard of experiments using liquid dishwashing detergent as a fungicide. Since they had a hedge heavily infested with powdery mildew, they decided to do their own tests.

They sprayed their side of the hedge with Dawn, putting 4 tablespoons of detergent in a hose-end sprayer, which gave them a ratio of 1 teaspoon per gallon of water. The neighbor on the other side of the hedge sprayed using a traditional chemical fungicide.

They sprayed with the soap solution every morning until all the mildew was gone. The neighbor sprayed the fungicide as directed on the package. On the sudsy side, the mildew disappeared entirely and stayed gone for three weeks.

The fungicide was not as effective; the relief it did provide did not last as long and it cost a lot more. The experimenters had no indication that the brand of detergent would make any difference.

 My coral bells have developed irregular, shiny, rust-colored spots on many of the leaves. What causes them and what should I do?

 Our first guess would be scalding caused by the hot sun hitting water drops on the leaves. Coral bells are among the plants with hairy leaves, which seem to be particularly susceptible to this sort of injury. We have noticed the same sort of spots on our bean plants.

If not too many leaves are affected, remove any with the spots, then watch the plants for a while to see if the spotting continues. If there are too many injured leaves to remove, just watch to see if the spots grow or if more leaves become involved. Check carefully to see if there is a chance the leaves could have had water droplets standing on them in the sunshine.

Of course there is a possibility the spots could be caused by disease — maybe fungus. However, more than half of plant problems are caused by a physical injury rather than by disease. Any time you have something wrong with a plant, think first, "Has it been injured?" The chances are better than 50-50 that it has.

 Can a marmot be a pest in a garden? I never thought such a cute thing could cause trouble until I saw one eating my strawberries.

 You are going to have to decide if you want cute or strawberries. See if you can borrow a live trap from the Extension Service, or buy one. Or you can use another kind of trap or a shotgun, but if you want any kind of garden, you have to evict the marmot.

If you live trap it, re-introduce it to the wild and not to someone else's garden. Take it several miles away or it will be back, a much wiser woodchuck, and it will be very hard to convince it to walk into that trap again.

We don't know of any effective barrier to marmots that isn't an awful lot of work and pretty expensive. You need to completely fence the area with several inches of wire underground and 1-2 feet above ground. Three-foot-wide chicken wire with part buried underground would probably do it.

A man in Pennsylvania reportedly heard that lion urine was an effective rodent repellent. He was able to procure some from a zoo, but a steady supply was hard to come by. Living in an area remote enough to ensure privacy, he experimented with human urine and found it to be equally effective, and he kept applying it regularly. However, after a week's absence, he found the rodents had returned. So if you try that method, know that it must be done on a regular basis.

 How do I know when it's time to tie up my cauliflower and what's the best way to do it?

 There is self-blanching cauliflower that doesn't have to be tied up, but it tends to be rather purple, like Burgundy and Violet Queen.
For the traditional white cauliflower, it is necessary to keep the sunlight off the head. The normal cauliflower color is a dirty yellow. This does not affect the taste or nutritional value, but it is our idea of serious ugliness.

The easiest way to keep the head covered is to gather up almost all the leaves and tie a string loosely around the bundle at whatever height will keep the leaves vertical. Enough of the inner ones flop over to keep the sun off the head. You also can fold a few leaves over the top and hold them in place with a spring clothespin.

To decide when to tie up your cauliflower, stand directly over it and look straight down into the plant. When you can see any white, it's time.

After a plant is tied up, check it at least once a week until the head is decent size. After that, check every day or two. The part you will be eating — the head — is a big cluster of flower buds. You want it to be as large as possible, but you don't want the buds to start spreading apart.

Why should I buy a lawn mower with a blade that chops up clippings and spreads them on the lawn and then buy a special rake to get rid of the clippings so they don't become thatch that kills the grass?

 You are working from misinformation on what thatch is. Thatch is a thin layer of matted, dead grass and dead grass roots that your lawn's roots have to grow through. Thatch is like putting a waterproof fabric on the ground and planting grass seed on top of it. The roots can't get through to the soil.

Thatch comes from watering too frequently and in too small amounts, from over-fertilizing and from cutting the lawn too short. It does not come from using a mulching lawn mower.

We recommend buying a mulching blade for your lawn mower and saving the rake money to spend on something else. For most lawns, thatch rakes are a snare and a delusion. All they do is remove the end of last year's grass before you start mowing the new grass.

The only reason to remove dead grass in the spring is because you can't stand the looks of it, or you need the exercise. If the old grass is unsightly, you might rake it off and use it as mulch in your flower beds. Having overwintered, its nutrients already have been leached away, but its physical structure is still valuable as a soil conditioner.

If you let your grass get too long before mowing, it might not be chopped up as well by the mulching blade. But chopped clippings are not thatch. They are a source of fertilizer for your lawn and will provide from 50 to 100 percent of the nitrogen needed.

The whole idea of mulching grass clippings has been around for a while—long enough to get to Montana and long enough to be given the name of ''grasscycling,'' and to be used successfully on golf courses.

We can't guarantee, however, that 50 years from now someone won't be writing garden columns saying the idea is all wrong. In the 1960s, the experts were sure that grass clippings caused thatch and you should rake them all up and rake the lawn thoroughly every spring. But at the end of the decade, a study done at the University of Rhode Island showed that to be false.

The Connecticut Agricultural Experiment Station was trying to find out if clippings do indeed provide nitrogen and, if so, how long it takes. Researchers used radioactive isotopes to track the nitrogen in the clippings and discovered that the cut grass began to decompose immediately. Within one week, the nitrogen with radioactive isotopes was showing up in the living, growing grass blades.

The University of Kentucky conducted a study of earthworms and thatch from which they concluded that the more you "manage" your lawn, the better your chances of winding up with thatch. The study showed that if you have a healthy population of worms you are unlikely to get thatch.

A major contributing factor in thatch buildup, the research showed, was not enough decomposition going on at the surface. However, if enough worms were present, they came to the surface to eat, speeding up decomposition, providing aeration and pulling organic matter down into the soil from the surface.

So if you are going to put chemicals on your lawn to kill things, don't use Sevin, Turcam, Benomyl or others that kill the worms. 2,4-D can be used to kill broadleaf weeds without endangering the earthworms.

 My son's lawn has white grubs and the store recommended a strong insecticide, which they admitted might not be all that effective. He has kids and dogs that play on the grass and doesn't want to use that stuff anyway. Is there any other answer?

 The damage you described sounds like white grubs, all right. When you can lift a chunk of grass off the dirt, it's because all the roots are cut off — that's what white

grubs do. They are a quarter- to half-inch long and are all larvae of a beetle of one kind or another. Books may tell you that
they are Japanese beetles, but in Montana, they are not—we
don't have to worry about those here.

Instead of asking, "How can I kill this pest?" you need to
ask, "Why is my lawn so unhealthy?" Every lawn probably has a
few white grubs, but if the turf is healthy, experts say you can
have 10 to 15 grubs per square foot and not have symptom one.

The most common causes of ill health in a lawn are compaction, cutting the grass too short and poor watering practices.

Compaction may be due to heavy traffic. If that's the
case, why not just stop trying to grow grass there? Plant flagstones instead. It might also be a lack of topsoil and lousy subsoil. If your lawn is fairly new and you put it in without tilling
thoroughly and making sure you had good soil, you may have
planted in the stuff your builders left behind. In an older lawn,
worms and ants have had a chance to move in and take care of
compaction. Work on compaction by aerating, which encourages the good guys to immigrate.

Your lawn should be cut no shorter than 2 inches—if it's
fescue, it should be up to a half inch longer. In cool, cloudy conditions, this doesn't matter so much, but in hot, dry weather,
you need enough grass to shade the soil. Also, grass must have
sufficient blade surface above the crown to be healthy.

Watering needs to be deep and infrequent to encourage
deep, healthy roots. Grasses that make good lawns in this area
do fine if you let the top inch of soil get dry before watering, and
proper watering prevents thatch buildup.

You need to control the number of white grubs, but don't
aim to kill them all. There are several diseases that attack them,
so you want to leave enough of them to get sick and re-infect others. Besides, if you kill all yours off, immediately others will
move in from your neighbor's yard, where it's overpopulated.

Although several insecticides say they kill white grubs,
a study at Colorado State University showed that aeration with
spiked sandals worked better than any insecticide tested. Walk-

ing over the infected area three to five times will kill about half the grubs, the report states, and provides an average of two spike holes per square inch.

There are a couple of biological controls for white grubs—milky spore disease and parasitic nematodes. Milky spore disease comes dry and is dusted on the grass. It takes about a year to see results, so put it on and look the other way until next season.

Parasitic nematodes are mixed with water and sprinkled on the lawn. Soil temperature needs to be at least 70 degrees, and you water the grass first to allow the nematodes to enter the soil and again after application to wash them down into the dirt. Don't apply too late in the season—they have to have time to get the grubs this summer because they do not overwinter here.

For those uncertain that their problem is white grubs, there may be other explanations. If brown spots are caused by disease, they turn up overnight and there is usually a pattern to the damage. Grass diseases are rather uncommon around here.

Drought also can cause brown circles that gradually spread. If you suspect the latter, water well and see what happens. If it's drought, the grass is probably not dead and will come back quickly.

 All of a sudden, a dead spot about nine inches in diameter has appeared in my lawn. What could have caused it and will more appear?

 The size and suddenness of its appearance are enough to give us the strong suspicion that your lawn has been watered by a female dog or a puppy.
Georgianna always thought there was something particularly toxic in the urine of female dogs, but Molly points out that males' urine has the same effect—the dead spots just appear at the bases of fence posts, trees and tall plants! Females and puppies squat and leave a concentrated puddle on a flat surface.

 Everyone I talk with seems to have another method for dealing with fairy rings. What's the best way to get rid of them?

 Short of hiring someone with a backhoe and a dump truck to come and haul away your yard, you really can't get rid of fairy rings.

Fairy rings are mushrooms of one kind or another, but the mushrooms are just a tiny part of the organism. The part below ground — the mycelium — is much bigger and there is no point in trying; you can't get rid of that.

Eventually your fairy ring will just disappear. It would be unusual for one to hang around longer than five years. In the meantime, there are two things you can do to disguise it.

The grass inside the ring looks bad because the mycelium is stealing all the water, so really sock the water to that area. Give it enough so that no matter how much the mushrooms use, there will be some left for the grass.

Another way to make it less noticeable is to sprinkle some quick-acting nitrogen inside and outside the ring, but not on the ring itself. The quick greening will blend the darker ring in with the rest of the lawn.

 The spot of moss in my lawn just seems to be getting bigger — what can I do to get rid of it?

 Your first step is to figure out why the moss is growing in that particular spot. The moss itself is not the cause of the problem — it is the result of a problem.

The moss is growing there because the grass can't. Grass is tough stuff and will outcompete most things, including moss, if growing conditions are satisfactory. There are chemical treatments that will kill the moss but they won't make grass grow in that spot unless you improve conditions.

The most likely reasons for the failure of grass to thrive in that spot are poor soil quality, excess moisture and insufficient sunlight. If it is only the latter, the solution is relatively easy. Just scratch off the moss, loosen the soil a bit and reseed the area with a shade-tolerant variety of grass.

Fescues, including red, chewing, sheep and tall fescue, are good choices. Tall fescue has a wide blade and the others are fairly fine. If you buy a mixture, read the label and get one with a high percentage of fescues and a low percentage of perennial rye grass, which tends to die out fairly quickly in this area.

If moisture is the problem, you may just be getting the area wet too often. Scratch up the spot and reseed, but also change your lawn watering habits to water deeply and less often.

If the wet conditions are caused by a drainage problem, like a low spot, a slant down toward a building or a layer of clay near the surface, you need to do more.

If you think you may have a drainage problem and aren't sure, dig a little hole a few inches deep in the affected area. Fill it with water, let it drain out and fill it again. Time it to see how long it takes for the water to drain out after the second filling. The water level should go down 1-2 inches in an hour's time, at the minimum.

If a clay layer is the culprit, you may discover it when you dig your test hole. The clay will be a different color from the rest of the soil—usually a bluish-gray—and it will feel slippery between your fingers. Probably all you will need to do in this case is to dig up the soil, break up the clay layer completely and mix well with the better soil and some organic matter. Then re-seed the area.

If you have a low spot, add topsoil to give the area a slight rise, then reseed. You can add topsoil gradually, half an inch at a time, allowing the grass to come up well before adding more. If you use that system, you won't have to reseed.

You may just have an area of soil that lacks nutrients. In that case, add good topsoil and manure. For lawn problems, chemical fertilizers are not the best answer—go with organic stuff that will contribute to the long-range health of the soil.

If you have healthy soil, lawns are one of the things around here that should never need fertilizing. If you do fertilize your lawn, you want nitrogen and not much else. If using chemical nitrogen, be sure it's the slow-release type. The cheap, quickie ones will leave you with more problems than you started with, like thatch.

Thatch is dead grass at the base of your green grass. It is mostly good and you don't want to get rid of it unless it is at least half an inch thick. Removing thatch is like putting compost on your garden and then removing it.

Thatch is only a problem if the roots of the grass are growing in it and not in soil. To test if this is the case, grab a good handful of grass and pull. If it lifts like a rug coming off the floor, you have thatch problems, but if the grass is firmly attached, you don't.

 What can I do to get rid of the moss in my perennial beds?

 We have talked at some length about moss in lawns; moss in your perennial beds will respond to the same basic treatment. If you have moss, don't think about how to get rid of the moss—it's just the symptom, not the problem. Think what you can be doing to get your soil healthy. The most common things to check for include poor drainage, overwatering, nutrient-poor soil and excessive shade. The things you decide to do to get rid of the moss are almost certain to make life better for your perennials, too.

My delphinium always have been beautiful, but this year their stalks are skinny, and over a three-week period the leaves have been turning yellow. What have I done?

 It may be that your plants have just run out of nutrients. Delphinium are fairly heavy feeders. Try giving them a dose of organic fertilizer, like fish emulsion, once a week for a month, or a shot of commercial fertilizer once a month and see if they start to pull out of it. Mark the dates of application on your calendar so you can keep track.

We hate to be the bearers of bad tidings, but it also may be that your delphinium are dying. They're not particularly long-lived.

 Do delphiniums bloom only once?

 They have one central blooming season, with large spikes on the main stems. But if you cut off those blooms when they fade, you can have a very nice secondary bloom. You get some blossoms on the side stems anyway, but removing the faded central blooms gives you a much better repeat bloom.

In a longer season, you get more side blooms. Also, there are many different cultivars and some are better at secondary blooming than others.

Garden books may say to allow not more than three bloom stalks per plant to get really good blooms, and if you are aiming for the ultimate flower to enter in a show, you must disbud a lot. But we haven't found that to be a good practice. A fatter clump helps protect delphinium from the wind.

Most of the information in gardening books comes from the Northeast, where wind is less of a problem. Eastern gardeners also need to keep their clumps thin and airy to avoid delphinium diseases that thrive in their damper climate. In our dry climate we don't have to worry about that.

 What's on maple trees around town? They're dropping their leaves and they're sticky. One of those maples is in my backyard. Is it dying?

 It sounds like aphids or some other little sucking bugs. After looking at the tree we found it was aphids, but the tree was in no danger. It had lost a few leaves, but not enough to cause any real harm.

The sticky stuff is called honeydew and that is what ants are after when they "farm" aphids on your plants and trees.

Georgianna is not bothered by one, or a few, of any insect or arachnid, but undergoes a terrible personality change when confronted by huddled masses of aphids or tent caterpillars. She has to do something destructive, which most seasons takes the form of overdoses of insecticidal soap applied to the aphids.

Aphids are fairly specific and the yellow ones on the maple trees will not move over to the garden and suck on your tomatoes. They may eat some other plant, but it will be something related to the original host.

If an 8-inch houseplant gets aphids, you may want to do something about it, but you don't need to worry about a maple tree unless it suddenly drops all its leaves.

If you are squeamish about aphids and are driven to eradicate whatever you have, you must be prepared to deal with succeeding generations ad nauseum. Aphid generations seem to be only about a week apart and, although the insecticidal soap kills them, in several days the plants are infested again.

You should know the difference between live and dead aphids. Dead ones don't look like aphids any more, but like tiny wads of gray-white lint. If you have those, save the insecticidal soap for the next hatch.

It is tempting to drag out the systemic chemicals and blast the disgusting little vampires into oblivion. However, one must resist. Aphids have a fair number of natural enemies. Spiders enjoy aphids a la carte and ladybugs are great aphid-gobblers.

If you must take up arms against them, see what you have that is mild. Aphids are slow-moving and soft-bodied and hence, easy to kill. If you drag out the big guns you end up killing your allies, the beneficial bugs.

We seem to have an especially large aphid population some years. Maybe they are here to remind us how lucky we are to live in this climate. When you are cursing the cold, or sick to death of irrigating, think of all the bugs we *don't* have.

 Last year we had aphids on our cabbages and corn although they didn't seem to cause much damage. Do aphids live over winter in the soil? Is there an environmentally safe way that we can prevent an infestation in this year's garden?

Aphids overwinter as eggs in cracks and crevices in the soil, and it is important that you remove from the garden any debris from plants that had aphids. However, the fact that aphids were bad one year doesn't mean they will be bad again the next, and it is unusual to have them on the same crop two years in a row.

Nobody knows how many species of aphids there are worldwide but there are thousands. Most kinds use only one or two plants as hosts and only about 10 percent aren't so fussy.

The heaviest outbreaks occur at the beginning and the end of summer, probably because at those times the plants have their highest nitrogen content and aphids love nitrogen.

When you see aphids, don't panic. Watch for a few days. If they suddenly multiply to the millions and look like they're going to suck the life out of the plant, then you need to do something.

Your best defense is to encourage lots of insects in your garden. Natural enemies will usually keep aphids in check and it is not often that you have to do anything at all.

You have probably heard that ladybugs eat aphids, but it is also the ladybug larvae that eat them. The larvae are not pretty, so don't go around the garden killing all the homely bugs. Ladybug larvae are orange and black, half an inch long and look like lumpy, wrinkly, ugly potato bug larvae.

Lacewing flies and birds also eat aphids but the best predators you are never going to see because the solutions to your problem are inside the problem.

They are parasitic wasps and the biggest ones are the size of a pinhead. The females lay an egg in an aphid — lots of eggs in lots of aphids — and when the eggs hatch, the larvae eat the aphids from the inside.

When you spot aphids, check to see if they all look healthy. If you see some that are different colors or are shiny or seem to be hard, leave them alone. They have probably already been parasitized.

If you decide you must do something, start by hosing the aphids off the plants. You will have to do this two or three times a week while you wait to see if other bugs won't come in and eat them up for you. You can also brush them off or squash them by hand. (Molly wears gloves for this process; Georgianna does it with her bare hands, but that's just a personal power trip.)

If you're not getting anywhere and the aphids are still multiplying, spray with insecticidal soap. You might also try one of the new summer oil sprays.

Like the old dormant oils, these products kill soft-bodied insects by clogging up their pores and smothering them. They also clog pores of leaves, which is why they must be used while a plant or tree is dormant.

The summer oils are so highly refined that they can be used on non-dormant plants. Just be sure to check the label to make sure you are buying a summer, rather than a dormant, oil spray. And remember, they are still considered experimental.

The important thing is not to get heavy-handed with insecticides and kill off all the bugs in your garden because the vast majority of them are beneficial and provide the best natural control of the harmful ones.

If you have aphids that a colony of ants is protecting, get a tube of Tanglefoot and use according to directions to keep the ants from getting to the aphids. Not only do the ants keep the aphids thriving, but they do their best to destroy the natural enemies that would kill their aphid "cows."

We have tried the experimental, homemade oil spray on aphids and it has worked very well. It got a lot of them on the first spraying and finished them off on the second go-round.

We mixed 1 cup of cooking oil with 1 tablespoon of dishwashing liquid and used 1-2 teaspoons of this mixture per cup of water for the spray.

 I have a brand new asparagus bed and the asparagus beetles have already discovered it. How do you handle them?

 As with so many pests, it's not the adult but the larvae that do the damage. Although you may see other beetles on your asparagus, the ones that do the harm are the ten-spotted asparagus beetle.

They are black beetles about a quarter-inch long, skinny, with red-and-white spots. They lay eggs in lines on asparagus stalks. The eggs look like black threads 1/16 inch long and sticking straight out from the stem.

The larvae are gray with black heads, and repulsive. They can get to be half an inch long if you let them live. Don't use pesticides if you can avoid it because you want to eat the asparagus. Insecticidal soap doesn't seem to have any effect on the beetles or larvae.

We haven't had a chance to try them yet, but this might be a good chance to employ the new horticultural oils. They could be sprayed on the pest at any stage — eggs, larvae or adult beetles. Horticultural oils kill by smothering. They would kill any beneficial insect who happened to be present at the time of spraying, but not those that came along after. They are not harmful to birds and can safely be sprayed on food crops right up to the day of harvest.

If you have just beetles and not yet worms, and if it's not a very heavy infestation, you can control them by catching the beetles and wiping the eggs off the stems. The adults are hard to catch when it's warm because they fly quickly, but in cool times of day you can get them. Keep an eye on the plants even after you stop picking — there could be another beetle outbreak about July.

A reader with asparagus and asparagus beetles wrote us: "Have had good luck with Bt on the beetle. Have soaked the ground around the plants in early spring. Also treat again about two or three times during the summer. So far they haven't come back."

We are delighted to know that Bt works.

Bt stands for *Bacillus thuringiensis*, which is a natural bacterium deadly to caterpillars and nothing else. It was developed to control the gypsy moth and has been available to home gardeners for about 10 years. As more gardeners experiment with it each year, they find more and more kinds of caterpillars it kills.

It works if sprayed directly on the caterpillars or on the leaves they eat. It paralyzes the gut and the larvae stop eating within hours. They don't die immediately, so if you go back the next day and find the worms still there, don't drag out the big guns and zap them. By the third day, they will be turning brown; meanwhile, since they have stopped feeding, your plants are safe.

Bt is available as dust as well as liquid. A couple of the names under which it is sold are Dipel and Thuricide. Because it kills only caterpillars, it will not harm birds who feed on the worms. If you have ladybugs, it will not harm them because their larval stage is not a caterpillar.

The only disadvantage is that you must wait for the right time — after the eggs hatch and before they become adults. It does no good to apply Bt at any other time. As long as the caterpillars are around, you probably should spray about once a week.

Being a natural bacterium, selective in its victims, it is also environmentally correct. Bt is a Good Thing.

 I have never had more than a few potato bugs before, but this year I have a zillion. I need help. Quick!

 The Colorado potato beetle seems to be more numerous in some years than in others. After the adults have been around for a while the larvae hatch and they are what does the damage.

The adults are really rather attractive — shiny black and gold — the sort of bug a jeweler might copy as a lapel pin.

It is highly unlikely that anyone would want to copy the larvae for any reason. They start out small — about a quarter inch when you first see them — and a dark coral color trimmed in black.

They grow amazingly fast, getting fatter, uglier and lighter colored.

Potato beetle larvae are the kind of creature, like slugs, that you instinctively want to squash into oblivion. Be warned that if you decide to do this you should do it at arm's length because they squirt a surprising distance.

If you don't have a great many, it is possible to control the beetles by picking them off and dropping them — adults or larvae — into a can of water with either a film of salad oil or a squirt of dishwashing detergent in it.

If you are extra-squeamish and can't stand to touch them even with garden gloves on, carefully position the leaf over the can and tap it gently. The bug or larva will readily fall off, whether the can is there or not, but once it hits the ground it's practically impossible to recapture.

If there is an adult, it has probably already laid a cluster of bright, yellow eggs on the back of some unsuspecting potato leaf, so if you can find any, remove them too.

Having thoroughly grossed you out with directions for mechanical control, we need to tell you there is another answer. *Bacillus thuringiensis San Diego* — Bt San Diego — is very effective and very safe.

Bt is a biological control. As we have said before, it is a bacterium that kills caterpillars only. You don't have to worry about getting it on your hands, killing ladybugs or honeybees, poisoning the birds that eat treated worms, or having it hang around in the soil.

The San Diego variety of Bt is so picky that it attacks only the larvae of the Colorado potato beetle. It is available under at least two trade names.

Don't apply it if rain is expected or just before you sprinkle, because it washes off and will have to be re-applied. Even in dry conditions, it is effective for less than a week.

Bt has been used on fields of potatoes for nearly 20 years and the beetles have not developed immunity to the bacillus so far.

 Each year I have an infestation of whiteflies on my Swedish ivy outside. I spray with insecticidal soap for a few weeks and they seem to be gone, but they always come back. What more can I do?

 The rhododendron whiteflies of western Washington, Oregon and California winter over there, but the greenhouse variety we have here are semitropical and overwinter outdoors only in the extreme southern United States.

Everywhere else they manage to perpetuate themselves very nicely in greenhouses. If you have whiteflies outside, they probably came on something you bought in a greenhouse to set out as bedding plants.

Prevention is the best way to control whiteflies. When you walk into a nursery, if you see a lot of them, back out quietly.

When you buy plants, check every single day for two weeks. You may be able to see the translucent young ones before they are big enough to fly.

In all stages, whiteflies live on the undersides of leaves. The eggs are too small to see and take 30 days to develop.

The young insects are so small you might not notice them until they start to fly and by then their damage will be done. Whiteflies can cause chlorosis, wilting, stunting and loss of leaves. They suck plant juices.

If you see even one, spray the plant with an insecticidal soap solution, a horticultural oil or neem, making sure you cover all surfaces. Keep checking frequently and spray again if more flies are spotted. Even if you stop spraying, do not stop checking.

A recipe for a homemade spray, developed in four years of trials by Dr. George Butler, was released by the U.S. Department of Agriculture. Looking for a safe insecticide you could make with things you have at home, Butler came up with: 1 tablespoon of liquid dishwashing detergent in 1 cup of cooking oil. This base is mixed at a rate of 1 or 2 teaspoons per cup of water and sprayed on.

Butler tested corn, cottonseed, peanut, safflower, soybean and sunflower oils in combination with Dawn, Dove, Ivory, Joy and Palmolive detergents.

The detergent is added to the oil to make it adhere to the leaves, but may harm the plant, so don't spray the only plant of that kind you have. Do not spray at temperatures over 85 degrees. Do not spray cabbage, cauliflower or squash. Do not spray in full sun.

If you decide to try this recipe, consider it experimental. Remember, if you are going to get leaf damage, you may not see it for several days.

Another thing you can do if you think you may have

whiteflies is to use sticky traps. The flies are most active at house temperatures. Look for them in early morning or at dusk when temperatures are cool and the light dim.

Whiteflies fly sideways, so place sticky traps to the side of the plant you suspect may be infested.

 I love gladioli and used to have beautiful ones, but the past few years they have not been nice. The foliage is yellow and the blooms deformed. Last year I got rid of all the bulbs and started with new ones this year, even planting them in a different area of the garden. They came up looking healthy, but many soon turned yellow and although most bloomed, the flowers were small and not pretty. Could it be thrips? Would a completely new flower bed do any good?

From your description, we can't give you the definitive answer, but we can talk about things glads can have and what can be done.
Gladioli are very fussy about getting lots of good sunlight. As trees and shrubs planted near them grow, you may be getting more shade than they will tolerate. They also need lots of fertilizer and should be given some at planting time and more when the flowers start to form.

It is basic to the culture of any annual or bulb not to keep putting them in the same place year after year—if you do, you are setting yourself up for trouble. If you find a place where they do particularly well, you could put them there every other year.

Many people plant glads in rows and use them as cut flowers rather than having them as a component of a cottage-type garden. You can create a monoculture by planting large areas of gladioli with nothing else with them. Try planting a few as a clump in one place and other clumps in other areas with other flowers around.

Glads come from corms which form a few new little ones around themselves and then die. Small corms produce small flowers. The best corms are supposed to be a half inch in diameter and deep, rather than shallow.

It is always possible to get stung when you buy them— you can even get stuck with bulbs that have the same thing the old ones had, so you might try a different source or two.

Weather also could have been your problem. The last few years we have had late springs with cold nights far into the season, which could damage the corms if they were in the ground then.

Thrips are a possibility, but you would have to have a very thick infestation to get significant damage. They scrape the surface, producing spots on the leaves before they turn yellow. Blossoms that thrips eat on look twisted and are likely to be streaked or mottled. If there are thrips on the corms, you should see red streaks.

To see if you have thrips, take a piece of white paper into the garden and shake the flower over it, then look for tiny black specks. Unless you have at least a 10-power lens, specks is all they will look like. In the case of a bad infestation, you could see dark specks that look like soot on the plant. That is fecal material, which is more visible than the thrips themselves.

Because thrips cannot live on a wet surface, frequent misting of your glads might help. Also, thrips have plenty of natural enemies, so try for a good mix of plants to provide homes for as many friendly bugs as possible.

Your glads might also suffer from a virus called "aster yellows." It gets its name because asters are its most common host. If you have grown asters or had carrot tops that turned yellow, immediately suspect yellows. There is no cure. If you decide that's what it is, the smartest thing to do is to grow no glads, asters or carrots at all in your garden for a year. Then throw out those corms, buy new ones and plant them in a new place the next season.

I never did get my spinach seed in the ground. Is it too late now?

 Well, it is both too late and too early. It is too late for an early crop and too early for a late one. You want your spinach to produce a lot of leaves, but in the long days of midsummer it will bolt to seed.

You can try for a late crop, planting in late July or early August. It is really hard to guess the timing for fall planting unless you have had experience. The weather is so unpredictable and we have so many different microclimates in the area.

Do not plant when the book says to plant a fall crop. It will probably be too late. Our best advice is to plant a few seeds from mid-July through early August. After that, there is no point.

There is no problem getting the seed to germinate at this time of year. The problem is to keep the seeds and seedlings cool enough. Cool-weather crops don't do well in hot weather. (That's why they call them cool-weather crops. See? Gardening isn't so complicated.) You can cover the seed with anything except plastic. You can even put a board over the seed and check every day, removing it once the seed is up.

If you are inundated with lettuce right now, it's a great time to plant a summer crop. Be warned that lettuce is tricky to germinate in hot summer weather. Curiously, old seed seems to do better in warm weather than fresh seed does. Don't cover the seed—just scatter on top of the ground and cover with floating row cover to conserve moisture.

Probably the easiest thing to do is to germinate six-packs of lettuce in the house. Once seed comes up, put the container outside; when the plants have four leaves, plant them in the ground. Put out a few plants every two weeks all summer long.

Consider planting a pinch of lettuce seed in half-a-dozen places around your garden or flowers beds every week or so all summer. Put it a foot away from anything else. In hot weather, it will grow in the shade. If it's planted in the sun, shade it until it is well up, then thin to one plant. You won't have a whole row the same age and you won't have so much you can't find enough neighbors to give it to.

 I have always heard that you can't move Oriental poppies, but I have one that must go. I would hate to lose it—isn't there some way to transplant it?

 Mid- to late summer is the best time to move it—after it has finished blooming and before it starts putting up new foliage. Poppy roots are notorious for falling apart, so don't be chagrined if yours breaks up into three or four chunks. You may replant the pieces as separate plants, or paste the clumps back together and plant as one. It may bloom sparsely next spring but will probably return to normal blooming the year after.

    Root division is the preferred way of propagating perennial poppies. When you move your poppy, try to get all the roots you can—at least 2 or 3 inches of root length. Any roots you miss will make a poppy plant next year.

    Most poppy roots are not quite as thick as a pencil, and they are brittle. Plant them vertically in the new spot and cover with no more than a half inch of soil. If you pack them in, you'll smash them all up, so use a light touch.

After many unsuccessful attempts, I have finally established some lovely pink poppies from my mother's garden and would like to share them with friends by saving the seeds. If I cut the flower stems off, will the seeds continue to mature in the house? If I leave them on the plant, do I also have to leave the unattractive, withered leaves?

We would like to say the answers are "yes" and "no" to your two questions, but it really must be the other way around. To successfully gather good seed, you must leave the flower head on the plant and the unsightly foliage should stay, too, until the seedhead begins to turn brown.

The good news is that you needn't leave all the flower heads on the plant. Each one produces so many seeds that, unless you have an unusually large collection of poppy-loving friends, one or two pods will provide all you want. Save the first couple of healthy ones and cut the rest off.

Bag the green seedpod with the toe cut from discarded pantyhose so you can watch what's happening in there. It will make seed faster this way and will get the air circulation it needs. Don't bag it in plastic, or it may mold.

Once the seedpod turns brown, you can cut it and put it in an open paper bag indoors to finish maturing and drying. This method of seed saving may be used for any type of poppy—annual or perennial.

I want some Oriental poppies that are not orange, but even the plants I have bought labeled as red or pink have turned out to be the same dark orange. Can I get what I want by starting some from seed?

Yes, it is possible to grow Oriental poppies from seed, although seed for any perennials may be hard to find. You might have to look through several garden catalogs. Don't buy seeds in color mixtures—most of them will turn out to be orange.

When you plant vegetables or common flowers you are likely to get what you think you're getting, but not always. Gardeners tend to get pretty philosophical about this. If you get what you want, great. If it comes out different but looks good anyway, fine—keep it. If it's nothing you want, compost it.

If you have bought flowers, shrubs or trees thinking you knew exactly what you had only to have them turn out completely different, you are not alone.

Gardeners are having a lot of trouble with mislabeling of nursery stock. Demand for plants has been increasing geometrically, but the numbers of experts to grow them are not growing that fast. Therefore, nurseries are hiring people who aren't all that knowledgeable just to fill the orders.

It is not a deliberate effort to defraud—at least not in most cases—and there doesn't seem to be anything we can do about it. Perhaps the best defense is a change in attitude that would allow us to say, "Oh, well. Purple is an interesting color, too."

Somewhat the same thing can happen when you get seeds or bulbs from a friend. They have something lovely they are willing to share with you, but you have a terrible experience with it. When you tell them about it, they say, "Oh, didn't I tell you you were supposed to ..."

 My Oriental poppy has begun to bloom again. Does this mean it is out of phase and will winter-kill?

 This is not an uncommon behavior among plants that bloom in late spring and early summer, and it doesn't seem to hurt them.
Oriental poppies bloom early, make seedpods and then go dormant. Their foliage dies, but in late summer they put up new leaves. Some of them will even bloom, although more do not.

The Oriental poppy (*Papaver orientale*) originated on the border of Iran and Afghanistan and was brought to France in the 1700s. Most poppies belong to the family *Papaver*. The oldest are probably opium poppies, which Greek myth says were created by Somnus, the god of sleep, so Ceres, the goddess of agriculture, could rest and be ready for her busy season in the spring.

Wherever they originated, they were flourishing around the Mediterranean that long ago.

The opium comes from the immature seedpods. The plants also produce the mature seeds we use for cooking; their oil is used in food processing and the cake left over is used for cattle feed.

It is illegal to farm opium poppies, but nobody cares if you have a few in your garden for the flowers.

Opium poppies (*Papaver somniferum*) are annuals that grow 3-5 feet tall. Some strains are peony-flowered and may be listed in catalogs as *P. paeoniflorum*.

The most common annual poppy is the Shirley, named for a British cleric, the Rev. Wilkes of Shirley, who spent most of his adult life breeding them.

He started with the wild corn poppy, which was red with large black spots, bred out the black spot and kept at it until he had white, pink and red flowers — even some bicolors. Shirley poppies grow very well here.

Iceland poppies (*P. nudicaule*, because their stems are leafless) are native to northern regions all around the world.

They are rather picky, so if at first you don't succeed, try, try again — but in different locations — until you find one they like.

They are a short-lived perennial or biennial, but self-seed freely and once they arrive at their favorite spot, they will make a nice clump for you.

P. alpinum is a cute little version of the Iceland poppy native to the Swiss Alps. Botanists know it was once native in other areas. It is known to have been in Great Britain before the last ice age, but it no longer is native there.

The California poppy is not a *Papaver*. Its secret name is

Eschscholzia californica, named for a German botanist who discovered it in the Sunshine State.

Like many other Californians, *Eschscholzia californica* has decided that Montana is a great place to live.

 How do I know when it's time to pull my onions and what do I do with them once they're out of the ground?

 The easy way to tell when onions are ready to harvest is that their tops bend over. If you planted all your onions at the same time and some of them are lopped over and some aren't, it's OK to bend the rest over. The old farmer's way is just to step on them.

Leave the onions in the ground for a few days—they will stop growing and their skins will start to dry. Don't leave them longer than about a week, or they will start growing again and won't keep as well.

When you pull them, do not wash them. You want to keep them dry. Dry is more important than temperature when storing onions, too. If you have a choice between dry and warm or cool and damp, opt for the former. Dry them out of the sun. If drying outside, cover the onions at night, so they don't get wet with dew.

Treat your onions gently—they will bruise, which impairs keeping quality.

Rub off as much dirt as possible. A fancy way to store them is to French braid the tops together while they are pliable. If you don't do that, wait until the tops are really dry and then remove them.

Walla Wallas and other sweet varieties don't keep for very long. They must be stored so they aren't touching each other. You can lay them on old window screens, or put them in mesh bags with a rubber band between them to keep them apart.

Have you ever wondered why you can't grow Vidalias?

If it is any consolation, they can't grow Walla Wallas in Georgia, either. The reason is onions' sensitivity to day length, so when you buy onions — either sets or seed — get ones that say they are a northern variety.

Southern onions in a northern climate begin making bulbs too soon, so you get only small onions. Northern onions in a southern climate get tired of waiting for the long days that trigger bulbing and just give it up.

Hotness in onions has to do with sulfur content, which also is what determines keeping quality. Chemical compounds with sulfur are what make onions hot, and lack of sulfur compounds is what keeps sweet onions from storing well.

 My little pine tree has white spots on its needles. What are they? Do I need to do something about them?

 The white spots you see are the dead adults of pine needle scale. It is merely a shell in which the creature's eggs hatched.

What does the damage is larvae, and if you are going to kill them you have to get them at their crawling stage. Hold a piece of white paper under a branch and tap the branch. If you can see reddish specks moving around on the paper, you have scale larvae.

Insecticidal soap is very effective against scale crawlers. If you know you have scale, mark your calendar for next March and when it rolls around, spray the tree with a dormant oil. The oil smothers the living organism under the protective shell to prevent the next hatch.

On the other hand, even though scale is endemic to the area, healthy, happy trees seem able to thumb their noses at it. Scale is a sign of a stressed tree. Is your tree getting enough sun? Enough water? How is siol fertolity? Is it in a place that gets road salt or a lot of exhaust gases? Is there any sign of recent injury?

If the white spots are a fairly recent development, you should be able to get rid of them by treating the scale and doing all you can to improve the tree's general health.

 Someone told me the velvety white spots on my mugo pine were scale. I don't want to use a potent insecticide so close to the house — what can I do?

 Nothing. Although what you have is almost surely pine needle scale, it would take an extremely heavy infestation to kill the tree. Pine needle scale lives in Montana and Idaho, and ornamental conifers are particularly susceptible.

So the good news is that you don't have to do anything to treat the scale. The bad news is that the tree, in all probability, got the critters because it is unhealthy. If you figure out what else ails it and correct that, the scale will gradually disappear.

There are many situations that can stress conifers. A common one is water. If the tree is on a drip system that was turned off too early, it may be getting too dry before the ground freezes. As we have mentioned before, it is important for trees — and other overwintering plants — to go into dormancy with damp soil.

Another stress can be compacted soil. Ornamentals are often planted very near walkways where their root areas are trampled. If that is the case, aerate the soil and keep traffic off.

The tree may just be in bad soil. If it was planted in marginal soil in the first place, it may never have been really healthy. To help correct that, put on a thick layer of organic mulch.

If you live quite near a road or street — especially an unpaved one — dust may be a stressing factor. It is important to keep conifers' needles rinsed free of dust.

Is your mugo in the shade? With the exception of junipers and yews, conifers require a lot of sun and do not thrive in shade.

Fall

CONTINUED NEXT PAGE

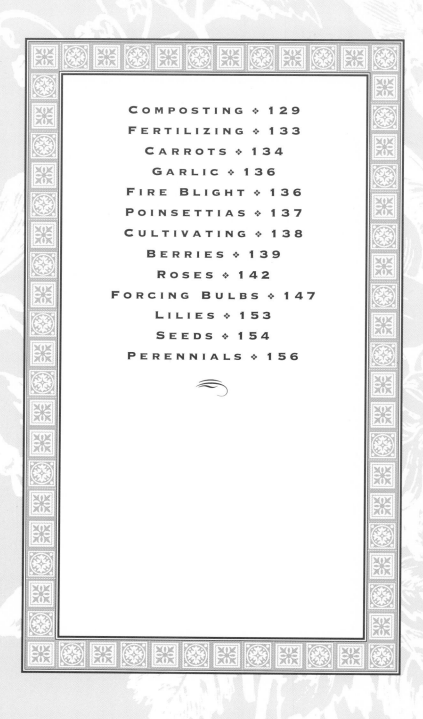

 I'm still watering my Christmas amaryllis bulb out in the back room and it seems to be enjoying its bloomless life. How long does this go on?

 If you plan to do something with your last-year's amaryllis, now is the time to change its regimen.

Quit watering it, tapering off over a couple of weeks if you want. Don't feel sorry for it when its leaves turn yellow and brown. Don't water it at all. The plant will not flower unless it gets a nice, dry season to be dormant in.

Remember, the bulb needs to be kept dry. Don't get all softhearted and decide to give the poor thing just a sip. It needs a minimum of three months without moisture to rest and regroup. If you water it, you cut off its interior monologue with itself and give it an incorrect message about where it stands.

Once it is dry, give it a month in a cool, dark place, then move it to room temperature. Don't water it too heavily until the sprouts are well above the top of the pot.

For basic amaryllis information, see the Winter section.

 What do I need to do to my summer-blooming tubers such as gladioli and begonias to save them for next year?

 The easiest things to save are gladioli, although they are corms, rather than tubers, and members of the iris family. You can wait until frost if you want, but you can dig the corms as soon as the foliage starts to yellow.

If you've grown glads for a while, you know that the corm you planted — the "mother" — will be in the middle when you dig it, with little cormlets around it. There will be two or three large ones that will bloom next year and several little ones that will take two or three years to bloom. The "mother" is dead and should be discarded.

It pays to keep your colors separate and label them.

Inexpensive, common varieties multiply fast — that's why there are so many of them. If someone gives you some of their extra glads, they're likely to be the common ones — red or white.

The fancy varieties aren't going to multiply as fast. They may produce only one or two big new corms and a few little cormlets. So save every last cormlet of the fancy ones and put in the compost pile most of those you have a million of.

All that glad corms require in winter storage is to be kept cool and dry. The best survival rate is achieved if they're stored at 40 to 50 degrees, but they can take a warmer temperature as long as they are kept dry.

The common method is to store them in paper bags, but you can also bury them in sawdust, vermiculite, perlite or dry soil. They need to breathe, so don't store them in plastic. A crawl space and pump house are possible storage sites. Most places around here are going to be dry enough.

Tuberous begonias are the next easiest to keep. It's best to dig them when a frost is expected. It's OK to let the foliage freeze, but the tubers are fragile and should not be allowed to freeze. After digging begonias, allow the tubers to dry before putting into storage. This may take as little as three or four hours or as long as a week or two. If your begonias have been out in pots, just leave the tubers in the pots. Otherwise, put them in a bag with some vermiculite.

When you store them, put them in a place you'll remember them. Check on them once in a while. If you discover one rotting, throw it out. If they are very dry, give the pots a little water or put a handful of water in the bags.

I transplanted two tuberous begonias from an outdoor planter to pots and brought them inside. They are still blooming. Do I have to put them in dry storage now?

 Heavens, no. If they are happy in your house, they will probably bloom for quite a while yet, and as long as they are healthy, there's no reason to upset their good humor.

Once they stop blooming and are no longer attractive, let them dry out and store them in a cool place, checking them every so often to make sure they don't get completely dry. The right amount of moisture is just short of shriveling. You want to find the fine line between so dry they die and so moist they mold.

 How can I keep my geraniums nice in the house in the winter?

 The primary consideration for geraniums is light — they need a lot of it. The ideal place would be in a greenhouse, as long as it is kept above freezing all winter. Geraniums love sun and cool temperatures, a combination hard to come by in the house during a Montana winter.

On the other end of the spectrum, you probably wouldn't be successful in overwintering your plants indoors if you have only a north window. Let's start with the assumption that you are greenhouse-less but have some space on a sunny windowsill.

If the geraniums are in containers outside, bring the whole thing in. If they are planted in the ground, dig them up, taking a pot-sized lump of roots. Knock off some of the dirt and plant in potting soil in a container. Put it in the sunniest window you have.

If the plants are blooming now, let them continue. You will have to prune them sooner or later, though. No matter how much sun they get, you can't give them long days, and they are going to get rangy. The internodes — the distances between the leaves along the stems — get longer when the plant doesn't get enough light. They get homely and too tall to fit your space.

You can decrease legginess by fertilizing only when your plant looks at you pathetically and complains that it is starving. Also, be sure it gets quite dry between waterings.

Geraniums are a plant that takes well to severe pruning, so don't hesitate to wade in and start clipping. Cut off all the straggles, plus a little bit more for good measure, cutting just above where a leaf is attached to a stem.

You can leave all the blossoms you want to. If your window is sunny enough, you may get blooms most of the winter, although it is more likely that as winter progresses the plants will stop blooming. How long a plant blooms depends not only on its location, but also on the variety and on its individual personality.

We recommend hedging your bets by rooting some of the cuttings you get when you prune. Trim the pieces to no more than six inches in length and remove all leaves from the bottom half. Let them air dry for an hour or more to let the cut places seal up.

Some people swear by one method of rooting geranium cuttings and some by another. Geraniums are notoriously hard to root. They would rather rot than root and if you get 50 percent to survive, you have done extremely well. Don't be surprised if rooting takes months. As long as the cutting hasn't turned to mush, leave it.

Molly prefers to root her cuttings in water and has found geraniums are one of the few things you can root on a sunny windowsill. ("Of course that's the way you do it," a friend in San Diego told her. "That's the only way you can keep them from rotting.")

In the spring, when it gets warm enough for your geraniums to live outdoors again, be sure you re-introduce them to the increase in light very gradually to prevent sunburn.

I have always just discarded my fuchsias at the end of the summer, but I had one this year that was too lovely to throw away without trying to save it over the winter. How is that done?

There are actually three methods for keeping fuchsias through the winter. The first is to let them go dormant. Bring them in and place them in a cool spot that will not get below freezing. A crawl space under your house is a good prospect. You can cut them back some if necessary to fit the space.

They will sit there, dry and woody, until you take them out in the early spring. One problem we have had with this is that, although the plants live and start up again, you are stuck with last season's woody stems and they may not turn out to be very attractively shaped plants.

The second method is to keep the whole fuchsia as a houseplant. Some have longer blooming seasons than others, and if the plant bloomed well this summer, you may get it to bloom for another month or more with morning sun. Try putting it 3 or 4 feet inside an east window.

A fuchsia will bloom all winter under grow lights if it is a good cultivar. In cool weather, be careful not to overwater. Although the soil cannot be allowed to dry out completely, overwatering can kill the plant with root rot. If this sounds like the voice of experience, it is. Never think that only you can kill a plant!

As the days become shorter, the stems between the leaf pairs get longer. Prune straggly stems any time up through March. Fuchsias bloom on new growth, and if you don't prune, you will end up with all your blooms hanging three feet below a leafy plant.

Probably the easiest way to ensure your plant's immortality is to take cuttings before it freezes. Although people with forest green thumbs may frown on rooting in water, fuchsias do very well that way.

Cut pieces 4-6 inches long, choosing stems that are not trying to bloom. Cut twice as many as you hope to end up with, because not all of them are going to survive. Remove the leaves from the bottom half. It is not necessary to have a stem tip, but you need at least four leaves. If you take your piece from the middle of a stem, be sure to keep track of which end is which and don't try to root the top end!

Once the roots are well-developed and healthy-looking, pot the plants individually in small pots. As soon as a stem has two pairs of leaves, pinch it out so it will branch. Keep pinching each stem as soon as it grows two pairs of leaves. When you're ready to transplant to a hanging pot, put three of the little plants together in an 8-10 inch pot.

If you have a terrible time spelling fuchsia, just remember that it was named for a man named Fuchs, a 16th-century German herbalist and professor of medicine. In the early 18th century, Charles Plumier discovered the plant in Santo Domingo and named if for Fuchs. The plants, which grow wild from Mexico to Chile, were taken to Europe, where they became one of the "in" plants of Victorian England.

 I have an old favorite ivy geranium that did not bloom well this year. Is there anything I can do to rejuvenate it?

 If the plant has been in its pot for a long time, the pot may be filled with roots and not have much soil left to nourish the plant. If you can handle an even bigger plant, you could re-pot it in a bigger pot. If you want the geranium to stay the same size, root pruning might be the answer.

Remove the root ball from the pot and, with a very sharp knife, take an inch off the bottom and an inch off all the way around the sides. Then put an inch of new soil in the pot, set the plant back in and fill around the sides with more soil.

Your plant will not mind being trimmed in this way.

However, it would not appreciate your taking the root ball in hand, manipulating and separating the roots, washing them off and putting them back in new potting soil.

We recommend that you take a lot of cuttings from your plant in case the old one continues to decline. Geranium cuttings are particularly prone to rot, so you will want to start with plenty. Put them in good, strong light, but not direct sun, and make sure they get good air circulation.

 My lawn is struggling. Is there anything I can do this fall to help it through the winter and maybe give it a head start for spring?

 If the fall weather is dry, you probably should be watering. It is very, very important for all plants — including grass — to go into winter with nice, moist soil. They have a tough enough time with all our winter freezing and thawing without having to contend with drought.

Grass grows well in cool weather and is probably growing more now than it did in August. With the cooler temperatures and shorter days, you needn't give your lawn an inch of water a week, as you did in hot weather, but it still needs some.

When your grass looks grayish, instead of bright green, it needs water. Another sign that it needs a drink is that it feels slightly crunchy instead of nice and soft when you walk across it.

Don't fertilize now. Although phosphate stays where you put it, any nitrogen applied now would be leached out by the time it is needed for spring growth.

If bare spots are a problem, there is no better time than now to plant. We should get fall rain and the seed should germinate before freeze up, getting a head start on spring by making roots now.

If your lawn has 40 percent of the grass you want, don't dig it up and start over — just overseed it. Broadcast the seed fairly heavily by hand, then scratch up the soil just a little bit with a rake. Grass seed should never be covered with more than an eighth-inch of soil. Then plan to keep the reseeded spots moist for several days. The critical point is the fourth day. Although the seed will not have sprouted, it will have reached its point of no return in the germination process, which begins as soon as the seed gets moisture.

With grass seed, you definitely get what you pay for. So if you're going to the work and aggravation of planting seed, get the best. Read the label. If you want a tough, drought-resistant, good-looking lawn, use a mixture with a lot of fescue. Bluegrass also does well here but is not as drought-resistant. Perennial rye grass does not do well here.

If you have seeded a large area, you will want to cover it with a protective garden cover of translucent fabric or a layer of straw for shade and moisture retention. Small spots in an es-tablished lawn should require only a daily sprinkling.

Lawns in this area will have to be mowed once — maybe twice — in the fall. The recommended height is 2½-3 inches. Leave clippings on the lawn unless they are so long and heavy that they will kill the grass under them.

The mulching mowers now available chop clippings up and spread them around. If you are shopping for a new mow-er, check these out. Kits also are available to convert a standard power mower to a mulching machine.

 I have heard that fall is a good time to start a new lawn — is it also the time to try to fill in bare spots in an established lawn?

 This is the very best time to work on those bald spots. If you do it now, the new grass has a chance to establish roots before the ground freezes, and it will have a head start in the spring.

First, figure out why the spot developed in the first

place. If it appeared suddenly and is less than a foot in diameter with dead grass in it, chances are it is a dog spot. You don't have to do anything at all; it will come back on its own in the spring.

Check for lack of topsoil, a common problem in our local soils. If the spot is rocky or a mixture of rocks and sand, grub some of it out and put in some reasonable topsoil with good organic content.

If you dig down and find a layer of clay underneath, check to see how thick it is. If it is shallow, you can poke holes through it and fill them with sand to provide needed drainage.

If the soil is compacted, break it up well and add some compost or sand to prevent the problem from recurring. If the area you need to repair is a compacted path, it is hopeless unless you move the path. Although the English have grasses that seem to thrive on foot traffic, our American grasses don't take well to being walked on. You might set some flagstones in the path and then plant new grass among them if the path is oft-traveled.

Once you have corrected the underlying cause of your bare spots, simply overseed the area.

 I want to plant a wildflower meadow. My husband burns the area every spring. When should it be seeded and what care do I give it?

 Fall is fine for seeding wild flowers. You needn't do a lot of preparation — just scratch the soil surface up as well as you can with a rake or hoe. Spread the seed thickly, water carefully, then keep it damp.

The area can be mowed or burned once a year, but it must be done in the fall, after the flowers have bloomed and gone to seed, not in the spring.

Leading you down the garden path:

In an article about making garden paths, we found a method that sounds interesting. It is called "soil cement."

You get a bag of cement and spread it on the soil, mixing it into the top 4 inches at a rate of one part cement to nine parts soil. If your soil is clay-based or contains a lot of organic matter, use one-and-one-half parts cement to nine parts soil.

Water it and compact it with a roller or by covering it with a board and walking on it. It takes a bag of cement for each 2 yards of path.

 Should I include fall-planted bulbs in my landscaping plan?

 This is wonderful bulb-growing country. You can have two months of colorful bloom next spring if you choose carefully and plant a variety. Back East, tulips tend to die out after a couple of years, but here we find ourselves digging them up every four or five years to divide them and trying to find enough people to give the extras to.

Bulbs and annuals make a great combination, but bulbs and perennials do not — they end up choking each other out. Bulbs are especially good with annuals you seed directly in the garden. Or you can plant seedlings of early blooming annuals and direct-seed late-flowering annuals. You will want to plant bulbs with something else because it's important to let the foliage ripen and it's nice to have something to cover the unattractive brown leaves.

Bulbs do well in full sun or mostly sunny spots and they like good drainage. They look best planted in clumps or drifts with at least three bulbs of the same color together, rather than a hodgepodge of colors planted single file.

Because your bulbs are going to be in one spot for quite a while, you want to have the soil in as good condition as possible when you put them in. To get them off to a good start, you can put about one-half teaspoon of superphosphate per bulb in the bottom of the hole. If you are an organic gardener, sprinkle in a handful of bonemeal for three to five bulbs. Be sure to use steamed bonemeal, or the dog may dig up your bulbs, looking for the bone. We speak from experience.

Generally speaking, bulbs should be planted at a depth three times the diameter of the bulb. This works out to about 6-8 inches deep for tulips, daffodils and hyacinths and 3-4 inches for crocus and other minor bulbs.

If mice frequent your garden, be prepared to replant your crocuses frequently. Crocus is the only bulb mice absolutely adore.

If you buy your bulbs locally, do so as soon as possible and either plant them immediately or store them in paper bags in the refrigerator until you can get them in the ground. They should be stored at 40 degrees or colder. If they sit too long in the warm temperatures of the store, they still probably will grow, but might not bloom the first year. Bulbs ordered by mail usually arrive at the right time for planting, but if you can't plant them right away, refrigerate them. Do not store bulbs in unventilated plastic; they are likely to mold.

Fall bulbs need an extended cold period. Those you plant now will spend the autumn growing roots and then require a long period of chill — a Montana winter. A little thought and care now will be handsomely rewarded next spring.

If you can't wait that long and want to force bulbs into bloom indoors when all outside is covered with snow, buy them now and pop them in the refrigerator. We'll tell you later how to have fresh flowers at Christmas.

Almost any single early tulip, the big hyacinths and large Dutch crocuses are easy to force. Species tulips, most narcissus and the small early crocuses are not easy. For forcing, get the biggest bulbs you can find.

It is important that you buy bulbs grown in cultivation. The catalog or package will say something like "grown from nursery stock," "field grown," or "we do not sell bulbs dug in the wild." Read the fine print.

If you care about the state of the wild, you don't want to buy bulbs that somebody in Turkey dug up a hillside to get. Harvesting bulbs from the wild has become a big problem in several areas of the world.

Our warning about mice adoring crocus bulbs was proven once again — this time in Georgianna's pump house. In a box of several dozen bulbs, the tulips, daffodils, hyacinths and amaryllis were untouched, but all that the crocus bags contained were some remnants of the papery outer layers and some mouse droppings.

Molly admits that it was only last year that she figured out why her own crocus patches weren't expanding as expected — mice were digging the bulbs for dessert.

The bulbs I ordered have arrived. Is it too early to plant them?

 No, it's not too early. And for those of you who did not mail order bulbs and plan to buy them locally, early fall is the time to get them — before the biggest bulbs and best varieties are gone and before they have sat too long on the warm store shelves.

There is a lot that goes on in the life of a bulb that we humans don't get to see because it takes place underground. During the fall, between the time you plant them and the time the ground freezes hard, your bulbs are very busy growing the roots that will enable them to support leaves and flowers next spring.

During this period, they need moisture, so water the bulbs at planting time and again later in the fall if they don't get a lot of rainfall.

If you can't plant your bulbs right away, keep them out of the reach of mice. This brings us to a discovery we recently made. If you are storing bulbs to force or to plant outside later, do not store them with fruit — especially apples. Ripening fruit produces ethylene gas, which damages the developing flower buds and may keep them from blooming entirely.

 Composting sounds like such a good idea, but why does it have to be so mysterious and intimidating?

 You are right — gardeners can practically make composting into a religion if they want it to be. However, it doesn't have to be that complicated. We will try to take some of the mystery out of it.

Composting is just letting things rot — it is taking the things that come out of the soil and putting them back. Peter Chan of Portland, Oregon, who writes on gardening and is an intensive gardener himself, says Americans are too impatient about composting. He's probably right — Americans are impatient about a lot of things. You know — "Lord, give me patience, and I want it right now!"

Composting does take a while — it will be a year before you get any finished compost at all and three years to get a reasonable amount. The wait is worth it. Nothing gets the results in the garden that a good dose of compost produces.

When you are just starting, you will treat your compost like the pure gold it is. You pick out the worst-looking plant, give it a quarter-inch and say, "Here, darling. Do the best you can."

There are various methods of composting, but it is always micro-organisms that do the work. They eat up plant materials and turn them back into nutrients. Your job is to make their environment as pleasant as possible. They need warmth, moisture and air.

There are anaerobic organisms that make compost without air, but compost made in anaerobic conditions stinks. Aerated compost has a lovely, earthy, natural smell. It looks and feels like the richest soil you ever saw — and it is.

You can put any plant material in your compost pile, but certain things — like raspberry canes, cornstalks, avocado pits and cabbage stems — decompose very slowly. You might consider putting that sort of thing in a "slow" pile. If you have heard that you should not compost citrus peels, try disregarding that advice. We find that citrus decomposes rapidly in this climate.

Check the bottom of the slow compost pile every year to see what's down there. Check the regular pile twice a year, probably once in the spring and again in the fall. Separating the materials this way saves labor in the long run.

A bad-smelling compost pile may be caused by either of two things — rotting animal material or keeping the pile so wet that it becomes anaerobic. Eggshells are the only animal product that can go on the pile. Do not include anything that contains fats, meats, fish, poultry, dairy products or bones.

By all means, put the rest of your kitchen garbage in the

pile — tea bags, coffee grounds, peelings, cores and the uniden-
tifiable slimy green things that sneak into the bottom of your
crisper drawers when your back is turned.

Of course, you will be saving your grass clippings and
other garden wastes. Green stuff makes nitrogen and brown
stuff makes carbon. You are striving for a balance, and do not
want all of either type. It's fine to add weeds, but it's best to
avoid any that have formed seedheads unless you are sure your
pile will get hot enough to sterilize them.

Warning! Don't put quack grass, no matter what its stage
of development, in your pile. It can survive anything and thrive
in the process.

Composting here is different from many other locations
because of the dry climate. It is best to locate your pile in at least
partial shade and to keep it as moist as a wrung-out sponge.
Keeping the pile moist in dry weather may be the hardest part
of the composting process. If you pile it up, eventually those
microbes will digest it for you. "If you build it, they will come,"
does not apply only to baseball players and cornfields.

Would you enjoy messing and playing with your compost to speed it along? You can sprinkle on some concentrated
nitrogen, like a quart of manure or a handful of chemical nitrogen fertilizer. Break, cut, chop or saw things into smaller pieces.
Turn the pile to add air and to let the microbes meet new friends
and form productive new relationships.

To get the temperature up, the minimum pile should be
the size of a washing machine. Anything smaller will still make
compost, but not as fast, and it won't get hot enough to sterilize
weed seeds.

If you want to keep your pile in something, you could
line a slatted wood enclosure with black plastic, leaving the bottom open. Or make a circle of wire and put in an enormous leaf
bag with the bottom cut out, or wrap the sides with plastic.

The big plastic barrels you occasionally see for sale outside grocery stores make fine compost bins. Get the kind with
the removable top. Cut the bottom out and drill lots of quarter-

inch holes all around the sides to let air through, and a few in the lid to allow rain or sprinkler water to drain in.

Consider, when choosing a container, how hard it might be to get the compost out from the bottom. With a barrel, you can just tip it over. Of course, there are commercially made compost containers which vary greatly in degree of fanciness and technology — and, hence, in price.

Once you find good stuff on the bottom of the pile, you need to sieve it. Half-inch hardware cloth stapled to a sturdy frame works well. Use the side of a trowel to mash the stuff through the wire — you can ruin a good pair of gloves in no time trying to do it with your hands. Anything that doesn't go through can be thrown back in the pile to finish rotting.

You can even compost in the house if you have plenty of room. You will need several five-gallon buckets, a little soil and some red worms. You have to keep transferring the stuff from one bucket to another as it rots and you have to keep the worms warm in cold weather. There is even composting-in-place. If the spot isn't right by your front door where every visiting friend, salesman and missionary will see it, you can pull the weeds or rake up the grass and leave them right there on top of the ground. It's best to leave purslane or other fleshy plants a day or so to dry out before adding them to garden beds. With large quantities of grass, give it at least a day to dry out. If it's green, make sure it's not wet.

Recent research at the Ohio Agricultural Research and Development Center showed that the more organic matter in the soil, the greater the ability of the soil to support friendly microbes, which eat up bad bugs and diseases.

Lots of compost will make plants healthier, the study showed. It provides nutrients for the plants and is a feeding ground for healthy bugs and microbes. Good bugs will eat up bad bugs if you give them half a chance.

The University of Florida decided to test the Ohio idea and planted beans and tomatoes in composted and non-composted soils. In the composted area, they reported markedly less disease and a 25 percent higher yield.

A local gardener did a similar experiment with his beets, composting half the crop. He reported an astonishing difference and said you could see the line between the plots as the plants grew.

NEXT YEAR STARTS NOW

Instead of thinking of fall as the first part of winter, gardeners see it as a necessary precursor of spring. When you have decent weather this time of year, you can do a lot of things that will make you very happy in the spring. Any weeding you do on a pleasant fall day saves you at least 100 percent more work in spring.

It is especially important to check edges where quack grass is trying to move in. Quack grass loves to grow in cool weather.

If you want to till, this is a good time to do it. Don't smooth it out — just leave it in big lumps.

Molly is of the no-till school. Her garden has done very well without it and her belief has been reinforced by an article by a man who hadn't tilled in 10 years, with good results.

Fall is not the time to fertilize with chemical fertilizers. Chemicals, especially nitrogen, will have leached out and disappeared into the nearest stream by the time you want them to do good things for you.

The exception, of course, is fertilizers that say they are "winterizers." They will either be very low in nitrogen or be processed for timed release.

This is the time when you can have a satisfying gardening session, turning and sieving and spreading compost to prepare the garden for spring.

Some of our compost containers are large plastic barrels. When we get ready to check the compost, we tip the barrels over

and start from the bottom digging stuff out. We may find wonderful compost a third of the way up in the barrel. But the most
pleasant surprise will be under a long-term compost pile.

This is where the raspberry canes, broccoli and cauliflower stems and corn stalks with their accompanying clods of
dirt have been put and have lain undisturbed for the past five
years. We have been able to trace three years of gardening by the
top layers, but below that is just pure compost.

After a reasonable period of gloating and some silent
prayers of thanksgiving, we spread garden-cart loads of that
brown gold on the vegetable gardens. It will be four or five years
before we can do that again, but we figure the wait is worth it.

We agree with Peter Chan, Portland, Oregon, gardener and
writer, whose philosophy is, "Why hurry? It's going to rot anyway."

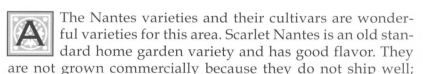 We grew two kinds of carrots this year and a lot of the
Scarlet Nantes were split and rotten. Is that not a good
variety to plant here? Why did this happen? How
should we store those that came through? Is it true you should-
n't store carrots with apples?

The Nantes varieties and their cultivars are wonderful varieties for this area. Scarlet Nantes is an old standard home garden variety and has good flavor. They
are not grown commercially because they do not ship well;
they are too brittle.

Your carrots split because they were post-mature — they
were left growing in the ground too long. After carrots reach
maturity, if the weather is still warm and they are still getting water, they keep growing and they have nowhere to grow but out.

The carrots rotted because they split, letting in fungus
and soil-borne micro-organisms.

In choosing a variety of carrots to plant, keep in mind
that almost nothing but the seed you plant has any influence on
the flavor of the product. Ninety percent of the flavor is deter-

mined by the seed, so you may want to try different kinds until you find one that you like and want to stay with.

There are several ways to store carrots, but all involve keeping the vegetables cool and moist. If they are kept in high humidity at temperatures below 40 degrees, they will keep until spring. You can keep them in a refrigerator or root cellar. You can even put them in a pit dug in the ground or leave them where they grew, but in those instances, they must be extremely well-insulated, as with broken bales of straw or other deep mulch. This becomes a problem when you want a few for dinner and have to dig down to get them and then re-cover the rest.

Storing carrots in plastic bags holds humidity, but poke lots of holes in the bags to allow the carrots to breathe — without this circulation, they will rot.

One solution to the splitting problem is to plant a few carrots in your early garden to be pulled and eaten during the summer, then to plant more three or four weeks later to be harvested for storage.

It may sound like an old wives' tale, but yes, it's true you should not store carrots — or other vegetables — with apples. Apples and pears give off ethylene gas, which ripens fruit but does disastrous things to most vegetables. It makes carrots taste funny — bitter — and is also bad for potatoes and cabbage.

Last year my garlic didn't keep well and a lot of it sprouted. What causes that?

 Your garlic was probably not through growing when you harvested it. If you are going to plant garlic in the spring, you must get it in just as early as you possibly can. It is better to plant it in the fall and mulch it with 5 or 6 inches of something loose like pine needles or straw to keep it from coming up in February when you get a couple of warm days.

Leave your garlic in the ground until the tops are brown almost all the way down to the bulb. The leaves won't fall over like onion tops and you shouldn't knock them down. Once you dig your garlic, let it dry, out of the sun, before storing.

 I had a lot of fire blight damage on my crab apple trees this spring. What can I do to avoid more next spring?

 There was a lot of fire blight this year. A bacterial infection, fire blight is most common in cool, wet weather. The bacteria turn up on the flowers and are spread by insects that pollinate the trees.

The bacteria are always around – the disease is not going to go away. Even if you eradicated the bacteria from your own trees, they would just spread to your yard from your neighbors'. Streptomycin sprays, applied when the tree is in bloom, may help temporarily.

If you're not sure whether your trees have fire blight or some fungus, don't worry about it. Treatment is the same. You must prune out the damaged branches, well back into healthy wood.

Pruning must be done before November is over and must not be done when the temperature is 18 degrees or colder. Pruning later or at lower temperatures results in cuts that will not heal because the tree is too deep in dormancy. Such cuts just provide another entry for pests and disease.

Before you make your first clip, prepare to disinfect your cutter after *every cut*. This must be done with either alcohol or a 10 percent bleach solution, by dipping the blades in the liquid or by rubbing them with a cloth soaked in it. Even though this is a nuisance, you must do it. If you don't, you won't solve the problem. In fact, you'll spread the disease. (If you disinfect with bleach, wash blades when you finish, to prevent corrosion.)

Prune branches damaged by fire blight 12 inches (yes, a foot) back from the canker. If there are cankers in places you can't prune—like the trunk—scrape the area back to healthy wood. The bacteria overwinter in the cankers.

The diseased wood must be handled carefully and disposed of completely. Burning it is best, but if you cannot do that, be sure to dispose of it far away from any susceptible tree.

Although apples are particularly well-known for susceptibility to fire blight, many other things are at risk. These include: pears, quince, hawthorns, mountain ash, serviceberry, cotoneaster and pyracantha.

If you are going to buy an apple tree, ask the seller if it is resistant to fire blight. Many varieties are less susceptible than others. If he doesn't know, don't buy your tree from him. No pear varieties available now are fire blight resistant.

 I saved my poinsettia and it's a healthy plant. Now, how do I get it to do its thing for the holiday season?

 Those of you who want to bring either a poinsettia or a Christmas cactus into bloom for the holidays need to put them to bed now. Poinsettias need 12 hours of complete darkness and Christmas cacti must be kept out of bright light in the evening. If your cactus is in a window, move it to a dim corner in a cool room. Cover the poinsettia with an absolutely light-proof box or shut it in a dark closet and don't open the door for at least 12 hours.

Be sure to uncover the poinsettia or take it out of the closet every morning. During the day it needs your sunniest window. The Christmas cactus will settle for some decent day-time light. September 25 is a good day to start the process for hol-iday season flowers.

Two notes on poinsettias: Studies at Ohio State Univer-sity showed conclusively that, contrary to a fairly popular be-lief, the plants are not toxic to humans. According to the results, eating 500 bracts wouldn't cause ill effects in a small child.

Although it is not yet commercially available, a new day-neutral poinsettia cultivar, "Eckespoint Freedom," has been de-veloped. It blooms in November, does not require long nights to bloom and is a naturally compact plant.

 To dig or not to dig: That is my autumn question.

 More and more, people are saying that the less culti-vating you do, the better. If your soil is healthy, you don't need to. If you are still trying to build it, you can mix stuff into the top 8 inches. This is probably a good idea if you have clay soil, if you think the surface needs to be broken up to allow water penetration, or if you want to break up com-pacted soil, like anywhere you have walked on it.

The main purpose of tilling is to expose as much soil sur-face as possible to the weather, so if you do it, leave the soil lumpy.

There are a couple of reasons not to cultivate. One is that you stir up weed seeds. Seeds of some weeds have been known to sit dormant for 25 years and then sprout once they are turned up into the light. So if you are rid of all the weeds on the surface of your bed, you don't want to "plant" any more.

The second reason is that once your soil texture is good,

with plenty of worms and beneficial microbes, you want to keep them as happy as possible and not stress them unnecessarily.

Some gardeners spread mulch on the garden in the fall and just leave it there, planting through it or moving some aside to plant in the spring.

Georgianna is rototilling as usual, but Molly is trying the no-till system. She has put compost on the garden beds and raked it around, but has not turned it over. Next spring she will rake it again and plant the area.

Rototilling, Molly says, is like hiring someone to clean your house and having them take everything out of the basement and put it in the attic. The microbes and beneficial organisms have their own favorite milieu, and when you turn over the soil, they have to start over, she feels.

 Are there things I should do for my strawberries and raspberries before I forget about them for the winter?

 There aren't many pests and diseases that afflict raspberries in this area, but strawberries face a lot of hazards. Some extra care in the fall can prove to be a big help in the spring.

First of all, clean the bed of dead leaves on the ground. Otherwise they will be waiting right there in the spring to be slug houses. Diseases and pests overwinter in dead leaves.

If your strawberry bed is 3 years old, it's time to take the plants out. It can be tempting to look at the big, healthy plants that produced so well for you this year and decide they'll be good for one more season, but be ruthless.

Strawberry plants always produce best in their second year and taper off a bit in the third, but after that the yield drops off so radically that you are wasting your time and garden space by keeping them any longer. This is the time of year to remove them.

Plan now for where you will plant your new strawberry plants in the spring. Once you remove old strawberries from an area, it should not be used for strawberries again for five years. Choose a new plot and prepare it to receive your new plants in the spring.

The 1- and 2-year-old plants that will be left in place may be clipped of leaves once they have turned brown. Be sure to do this if your plants have shown signs of strawberry leaf spot. Dispose of the infected foliage some distance from the garden and do not add it to your compost — the fungus causing the leaf spot survives the composting process.

We don't recommend that you try to grow your own replacement plants. If you do, don't save any but the "first daughter," the first little plant to appear on a runner. Those appearing farther down the runner get progressively smaller and weaker.

You're way ahead to cover strawberries with something. Molly throws a floating row cover over hers and weighs it down with rocks. You can also cover them with straw. You get much better crown survival, whether you have cut the leaves off or not, if they are protected from the severe winter.

Cane borers are about the only local pest raspberries attract. If foliage on isolated canes suddenly dries up, or if the canes start making berries and they dry up before maturing, pull straight up gently on the cane. If it comes right out, check the base — you will probably see a hole in it.

The damage appears during the fruiting season, but the time to attack cane borers is in October and March. We try to use as few chemical remedies as possible but with cane borers, it's time to get out the big guns. Diazinon is the only thing we know of that will get rid of cane borers.

Tell your nursery worker that you want diazinon for cane borers and check the label to make sure it can be used as a drench. It should be applied to the soil in fall and spring and must be done for two, or preferably three, years. The cane borer's life cycle is two years, adult to adult.

The adult is a clear-winged moth that looks like a yellow jacket, but rather than having the fine hornet-type antennae, they have feathery moth antennae. They are also less aggressive. We wish there were a way to get rid of them without nuking plants, but we haven't found anybody that knows another method.

You don't have to mulch raspberries. Just leaving their own leaves on the ground under the bushes seems to provide enough protection. For now, cut out the canes that fruited this year. Also remove suckers that have migrated out of the raspberry patch and the little short canes. Leave remaining canes long for the winter and prune them in the spring when you can see how much tip die-back you have.

 I have some first-year raspberry plants. Do I need to prune them off for winter?

 No. At least not most of them. The canes that made leaves this year are the ones that will make fruit next year. But any that tried to bloom and fruit this year are dead and should, indeed, be pruned out.

Raspberries are a perennial with biennial canes. Plants don't submit to categorizing as easily as people categorize them.

The dead canes will look gray-brown, as opposed to the red-brown of the canes that will fruit next season. To do it right, raspberries should be pruned twice a year. Prune the dead ones out now and remove any that are obviously short and spindly. If this is their first year, you will have very few to remove. Cut them off as near the ground as possible—you will not be thrilled to find a bunch of dead stubs when you start cleaning out the bed in spring.

It really doesn't hurt to wait until spring to do this pruning, but we prefer to do it in the fall. If you wait, you must do it early—before bud break. It also makes the plants easier to reorganize for winter, tying them up, staking and straightening them.

In the spring, you can trim the tops down to a convenient height for picking. We clip them to reach halfway between waist and shoulder, which is not where they will end up as the season progresses, of course. How much you cut depends at least partly on variety. Some need much more topping than others. If you don't trim the tall ones, they will be very hard to keep upright and will bend over and break the canes. With first-year babies, you probably will not need to trim the tops.

For the first winter, we would be inclined to mulch the plants like any perennial to protect the roots from sunshine. Cover them with something organic that will let air through. We like pine needles because they break down slowly, don't blow away and are easy to remove in the spring.

 My daughter brought me an old-fashioned rose called Van Fleet from her yard in Snohomish, Washington I'm afraid to plant it outdoors until spring. I have been keeping it watered and set it outside when it was sunny and brought it indoors now that it is cold. It is losing its leaves. Is this normal? If not, what should I do? I don't want to lose this lovely plant.

 We assume that your rose is losing its leaves because it is trying to go dormant. No rose will stay healthy forever unless it has some cool weather. You can't keep a rose at house temperature and have it do well.

If you haven't already inspected it carefully for insects or disease, do so now. If you find a problem, you can treat it before helping the bush into dormancy.

What you do with it depends on how big it is and what facilities you have. Find it a cool place, but tempered. A crawl space, a cellar or an unheated garage would be fine. You could even cut it back and put it in the refrigerator if there is room among the leftovers. Keep the soil just short of dry and do not fertilize at all.

While we are on the subject of roses, local growers have found that for tender varieties, the Styrofoam cones are not enough to protect them in the winter unless they are filled with something else with insulating value, such as dry leaves.

A winterizing problem here is mulching with something that packs down. You need a lot of air in mulch for it to be effective. Leaves tend to get wet and soggy and to stick together in mats. Things like straw insulate well, but tend to leave with any passing breeze; you end up with bare roses and a fenceful of straw. We find pine needles to be a better choice because they don't pack down and they don't blow away.

fter we gave an off-the-cuff answer to this question about an old-fashioned rose bush, we got to wondering about it and digging into books, magazines and other publications. We found several rose-related items worth sharing.

Our questioner said her rose was called Van Fleet, that it was pink and fragrant. There are many old-fashioned roses with that name because Walter Van Fleet was a very active hybridizer of that type of rose. The bush sounds most like one named Sarah Van Fleet, which is a semidouble, continuous-blooming, fragrant pink rose. If that is indeed what the bush is, it is hardy to Zone 3 and should do well here with minimal fussing.

If you are growing the most common types of roses — teas, grandifloras and floribundas — you already know how to winterize them. They need mulching, covering, protection not only from our cold temperatures but also from our rapid and drastic temperature swings and desiccating winds.

There is a whole category of shrub roses that are hardy to 40 degrees below zero. These are fast becoming *the* rose for northern climates.

All of a sudden, breeders became interested in the old-fashioned roses and in the last few years have raised a great many. A large selection of repeat and continuous bloomers have been hybridized.

The reason shrub roses and certain other plants are so hardy is that they have learned to transport water from their cells to the spaces between cells. Thus the cells shrink and the water between them can freeze without bursting the cell walls. This is something you can't teach just any plant to do, but the trait can be strengthened or bred into plants.

Although some of the shrub roses, like the popular Austrian Copper, bloom only once in the springtime, almost all of the Rugosa-type are repeat or continuous bloomers. Shrub types come in sizes ranging from over 6 feet to low ground covers.

In his book "Hardy Roses" Canadian nurseryman Robert Osborne lists no less than 18 pages of varieties hardy to Zone 4, and those are just the ones currently on the market and that he considers disease-resistant enough to bother with. He also has two pages of places you can order hardy roses.

Shrub roses are generally disease resistant, and Osborne says he doesn't spray with anything except a bit of sulfur for varieties particularly susceptible to black spot. He recommends spraying a mixture of one ounce of baking soda to 10 gallons of water on roses after a damp period as a preventive for mildew. He assumes it makes the leaf surfaces less acid and so less hospitable to fungi.

Once your rose has fungus, you can't get rid of it, no matter how potent your fungicide is. You must spray to prevent it, so as soon as mildew appears on a bush, be sure to keep spray-ing the bush's new foliage to prevent spread of the fungus.

Now a couple of notes on pruning roses. George Evans of Montana State University recommends not pruning your roses until spring. This was welcome news to Georgianna, who has always done it that way, but wasn't sure she had any official backing.

Q When should I cover my roses for the winter and what is best to use to mulch them?

A If you know a reliable oracle whose field is winter weather, it would be far better to consult him, or her, than us.

All we can do is give you our best guesses. We assume you are talking about tea roses which, along with miniatures, are tender enough to require insulation over the crown. You needn't wor-ry about the rootstock to which they are grafted because that is something extremely tough.

As we have said before, you are not trying to keep the bushes cozy warm all winter. It's not like putting the down quilt on your own bed. You want to keep them frozen, once they get that way. It is warm periods between cold periods that cause the roses to break dormancy, only to be killed by the next hard freeze.

Proper insulation will trap a lot of dead air space around the plant. You don't want the mulch to pack down and smoth-er the plant and you don't want it to blow away. The plant is dor-mant, not dead, so it requires air or it will die.

There are a bunch of things people try as insulation. One rose grower made cages of several layers of newspaper and filled them with leaves. You have probably seen whole gardens of Sty-rofoam cones, but nobody has been able to solve the ugly prob-lem: Styrofoam cones are just ugly.

Georgianna covers the crown a couple of inches deep in

dirt dug from another spot in the garden, then puts a cage of chicken wire around each bush and fills it with leaves. Of course this redistributes the soil in your garden, but it's not really that tough to remedy when you're readying things up in the spring.

Molly prefers pine needles for several reasons. She has a lot of pine trees to provide a good supply. They don't get soaked up with water. They let air through, but don't blow away. And they decompose slowly, allowing her to pick up armloads of them in the spring and to keep them handy in leaf bags for next year.

It is not time to mulch yet because the ground is not frozen, but this is a good time to collect the materials you will be using, whether it's pine needles, leaves, garden waste or something else. Put it under cover to keep it dry until freeze up. A few years ago the first snow beat us and lots of things ended up without mulch.

Another answer to the rose mortality rate is to plant tough, winter-hardy varieties which are not grafted. You treat them like any other perennial, which means mulch them the first couple of winters and then they're on their own. Even if the plant survives without mulching in its early years, it will do better if given winter insulation for a couple of seasons.

There are getting to be quite a few hardy roses. Many of them have long blooming seasons and many are very fragrant.

A local rose grower wrote an article for a Rose Society journal on the New Hampshire rose collar, a fairly new and very simple little structure for winter rose protection.

You want to end up with a cylinder, 15 inches in diameter and about 9 inches tall.

Begin with three or four sheets of newspaper, opened out flat and stacked. Fold the pile over in thirds, which will give you a flattened tube of newsprint, nine or 12 layers thick, 9 inches high and 23 inches long. Staple just enough to hold it together. Make a second one of these and staple their short ends together, overlapping, giving you the desired circle.

Set the cylinder on edge around a trimmed rose bush. After the first freeze, dump in whatever you have for mulch to a depth of 3-4 inches. Once the ground freezes, fill up the collar with insulating mulch.

We also suggest you try to put the Sunday comic section on the outside of your collars. Not only are they more colorful and flowery-looking, but having to look at depressing headlines every time you pass your garden could ruin your whole winter.

 Is it time yet to plant the bulbs I want to force into bloom for the holidays?

 Yes, if you're planting crocuses, hyacinths or tulips, but not if you're only planting paperwhite narcissus.
Paperwhites are very easy to force and are a great way to start if you are experimenting with forcing for the first time. However, they require no chilling time and will bloom in three to five weeks after planting, so if you want them in bloom at Christmas, plant them in mid- to late November.

If you already have the bulbs, keep them in the refrigerator in a paper bag. Be sure to protect them from getting squashed by other denizens of your fridge — they are developing sprouts that are extremely tender.

Whenever you plant any bulbs to force, you need pots with drainage and a good potting soil. Some directions for forcing will tell you to plant the bulbs in pebbles or water, but you will get more and better blooms if you plant in potting soil.

Four- and 6-inch pots work well. They don't have to be the deep ones — only about as deep as they are in diameter. These may say "3/4" on the bottom. There are also bulb pans which are even shallower.

You want the top of the bulb to be approximately even with the rim of the pot. Fill the pot about half full of potting soil and set in the bulbs at the correct depth and so close together they almost touch.

You can put a single tulip or hyacinth in a 4-inch pot, or

four to six crocuses. A 6-inch pot will take four to six tulips or three to four hyacinths. When the bulbs are in place, finish filling the pot with soil; it should just barely cover the bulbs.

When planting groups of tulips, plant with the flat side of the bulb toward the outside of the pot. The largest leaf comes from the flat side and curves out, so you will have a nicer-looking pot with a ring of leaves around the outside rather than a wad of them in the middle.

Water the planted pots and set them in saucers or in a pan. They now need to be kept cool and damp and dark. Temperatures should stay above freezing, but not above 40 degrees. Bulbs kept warmer than that will not bloom.

Minimum cold times are eight weeks for crocuses, 10 weeks for hyacinths and narcissus other than paperwhite, and 12 weeks for tulips.

Exceptions to the rules are the yellow varieties of paperwhites, "Grand Soleil d'Or," which is yellow with an orange center, and "Cragford," which is white with a yellow center. These bulbs will bloom in six to 10 weeks without a cool time, so if you have no cool place and can find these varieties, you can plant them in October for Thanksgiving or Christmas blooms.

Wherever you put the pots during the chilling period, make sure mice can't get to them — put mouse bait around or set a trap or two.

During chilling, do not allow the soil to dry out — keep it moist, but do not allow water to stand in the saucer or pan. The bulbs use this period to make roots. The times mentioned above are minimums for the species; to prolong your winter bloom you may want to leave some of your pots in the cold longer before bringing them out into the warm. They won't mind a long cold spell in the dark.

Once you take them out, they take three to four weeks to bloom. They will probably have produced sprouts, which is fine, but once sprouts reach a length of 5 inches, the pot must be brought into the warm.

Any paperwhites are fine for indoor blooming, and so are

the large hyacinths, and single early tulips and the large Dutch crocuses. If you have any doubt about the variety and the label doesn't specify, ask someone at the nursery which are suitable for forcing. No matter what type of flowers you plan to force, get the biggest and best bulbs you can find. Economy-sized bulbs just won't force decently.

For beginning bulb forcers, we don't recommend such flowers as Dutch iris, species narcissus and lilies because they need 40-degree nights after they are brought into warmth, which requires your moving each of them every day.

Note on your calendar when your potted bulbs are put in to chill so you can be sure you observe their respective minimum cold periods. As silly as it may sound, you do need to remember to plant bulbs pointed-end up!

If you can't face this whole process, get yourself an amaryllis or two. They are widely available in late fall, are not terribly expensive, are easy to care for and they will bloom. They are native to South America and attuned to the Southern Hemisphere, which is why they bloom in our winter.

 I'm a beginning gardener and have never tried forcing bulbs, but friends have told me paperwhite narcissus are easy. Are they a good place to start?

 Your friends are right—paperwhites are very easy. Unlike most bulbs, they don't require chilling or root-growing time. They already contain everything they need to grow and to bloom.

As long as you don't drown them or forget to water them at all, they will bloom cheerily about a month after you plant them.

As with the harder-to-force bulbs, we advise you to buy them as soon as they are available and refrigerate them in paper or ventilated plastic bags until you are ready to start them.

If they already have started to sprout, it's OK. Just don't

mash the sprouts or they will look crooked and ugly for the whole rest of the season.

Hyacinths also can be forced without a long period of chill, although they require a little different handling down the line.

The easiest way to force paperwhites and hyacinths is not to plant them at all, but to put them in special glasses or in beds of pebbles, marbles and so on, and let the bulbs feed on themselves.

As it says on food packages, "Just add water."

The object is to keep the roots, and only the roots, wet. If you water them too much, the bulb will rot. If you let the roots dry out, the whole bulb will shrivel up. This means that to start with the bulb should not actually touch the water — you just wait for it to put roots down to the water.

Special hyacinth-rooting glasses with wasp waists are just for this purpose.

You also can settle your bulbs in pebbles or marbles enough to hold them upright and keep the water level just below the bottom of the bulbs.

To get optimum results, give your bulbs something outside themselves to grow on. You can plant them in potting soil and fertilize as you do your other houseplants. (If you don't fertilize your houseplants, you probably should.)

Barely cover the bulbs with soil. It is OK to stick them partway into the soil, but by the end of the process, the bulb is pretty ugly.

If you plant hyacinths in dirt, they really need to be put in the cold and dark for a couple of months.

Some people start paperwhites in the dark, which gives them bigger root systems and makes them grow taller. But with forced bulbs, taller is not really better. Even started at room temperature and light, they will probably get so tall that they will need support. Hyacinths are an exception. Grown in any glass that holds the bulb above the water, they will not get as tall as the ones that grow out in your garden.

Paperwhites and hyacinths are happiest with quite a lot

of sun while growing, but not too high a temperature. They must have cool nights.

Paperwhites are pretty cheap. You could buy a whole bunch, store them in the refrigerator and haul them out to plant at two-week intervals. You could have flowers all winter to impress your friends, or to give as gifts. If you plan to give them as Christmas presents, get them out of the refrigerator at Thanksgiving. If you want to save them to brighten up your winter doldrums after the holidays, they will be OK in the refrigerator for a few more weeks. If they sprout in the refrigerator, be careful to protect them — if the flower sprout gets broken, you will get no bloom, and the sprouts are very tender and brittle.

Pots 6 inches deep and 6 inches in diameter are ideal for paperwhites. Although they will grow and bloom if planted in pebbles, you will get better-looking flowers if you plant the bulbs in good potting soil. If you're buying the soil, get the best you can find. "Best" usually translates into "most expensive," but high quality will pay off.

Arrange your bulbs close together — almost touching — and add soil to barely cover them. Water the pot. It should be kept constantly moist, but never allowed to stand in a puddle, or the bulbs will rot. Heft the pot in your hand — when it starts feeling light, it's time to give it a drink. Fertilize paperwhites as any other houseplant.

Place the pot where it will get indirect light. Once the tops are up, the paperwhites will want some direct sunlight in the day, but they still like a cool place at night. If you can give them such an arrangement, you will get more compact plants and the blooms will last longer.

At planting time, prepare to stake your paperwhites. It's not a disgrace if you have to stake them — with our short, often cloudy winter days, the plants are prone to lankiness. You can put in a small wire tomato cage, three green bamboo stakes or even a couple of natural branches. Then, when the stems grow up, you can confine them among the stakes with green string or yarn.

 I'm so anxious to plant my paperwhite narcissus — how do I know when to start them?

 It's fine to plant them as soon as you purchase them. Just figure on their blooming about one month after you pot them. Set them in good light, but don't put them in direct sun until the tips are well up and green.

Books used to say to give paperwhites two weeks in the refrigerator, but the current word is that if you don't do that the plants will bloom just as profusely and will be shorter — less likely to get top-heavy and fall over.

Molly tried saving paperwhites from year to year, as recommended in an English gardening book. She kept the bulbs in their pot in the cold frame until the foliage turned brown in August, then she removed them to a brown paper bag and put them in the refrigerator.

The hold-over paperwhite experiment was a washout. When replanted, the bulbs came up nicely, but didn't make a single flower bud. Call it misinformation, lack of skill or different behavior patterns in transatlantic bulbs. Call them additions to the compost pile.

Just when you think you have it right, based on information from authorities who told you exactly how to do it, along comes another authority who says it's all wrong.

Two recent articles on forcing bulbs recommended longer chilling — 12 to 20 weeks, compared with the eight to 12 weeks we have believed in for years.

OK. Count this up on your fingers. You pot the bulbs up in October and set them in the fridge behind the chutney. On the newly recommended regimen, they wouldn't come out until March. Then it takes three to four weeks after that before they bloom. What else is blooming then? Right. All the fall bulbs you planted in the garden.

Stay tuned. We'll see what they say next year. Never believe all you read — present company included.

I haven't planted my Asiatic lilies yet. The directions say not to wait longer than a week; it already has been 10 days and it's still very cold. If I plant them now, do they still have a chance?

 Definitely do plant the bulbs. Lilies can be planted later than anything else. Even after the ground is frozen, if you can make a hole for them and put an inch or two of soil over them, they will probably be OK.

Don't try to keep your bulbs over winter to plant in the spring or they will almost surely die. Asiatic lilies are sold in stores in the spring, but those were dug commercially in the fall and held over the winter under strictly controlled conditions of temperature and humidity.

Bulbs planted in the fall will do better because they grow roots until the ground freezes solid and will have a head start in the spring.

Lilies never go completely dormant, so they must be kept cool and slightly moist. When you order by mail, they probably will be shipped later than other bulbs. This is done because the weather is more predictably cool later in the fall. It is hard to keep lilies alive if they are allowed to get hot or dry.

Other fall bulbs — tulips, daffodils, hyacinths, etc. — must be planted deeper than lilies and are not hurt by being set even deeper than directed. Lilies won't come up at all if they are put too deep, but they have a built-in safety mechanism. Lilies have contractile roots with which they pull themselves down to a level where they are comfortable if they haven't been planted deep enough.

 I planted some lily bulbs this fall, but plan to make some new beds and rearrange things in the spring. Can I move the lilies then?

 Don't move the new lilies until after they bloom if you can possibly avoid it. Technically, you can move lilies any time because they have no period of complete dormancy, but these new ones really will not have had a chance to get settled. You would almost certainly lose a season's bloom, as the very least consequence.

If you move lilies in the spring, it must be done very early to avoid losing the season's bloom. As a family, Asiatic lilies are quite hardy here and make their flower buds at the right time for our climate. They usually bloom in July and August. Moving them after blooming gives the plants time to recover from root disturbance. Lilies' roots are fleshy and easily bruised, so it pays to take extra care when transplanting or dividing them.

 Seed is getting more expensive and I am wondering if it might be worthwhile to save leftover seed or to harvest seed from the plants I grew this year. Do some seeds save better than others? How long can I store them and under what conditions? How can I tell before planting saved seed if it's going to grow or if I need to get new seed?

Although saving flower seed is sometimes iffy, vegetable seed is easy to keep. Ideal conditions are 25 percent humidity and a temperature slightly below freezing. Vegetable seeds keep pretty well in the freezer if stored in a plastic container with a tight lid.

Each 1 percent drop in humidity doubles seed life, which is why you may have read instructions to put some silica gel in the container—about two teabagsful in a quart container. You can also use an equal amount of powdered milk in a paper packet. Seeds stored that way should keep for about 10 years.

The National Seed Storage Lab in Fort Collins, Colorado, was established in the 1930s and has reported some varieties put in storage at that time still have 50 percent viability today.

Generally speaking, open pollinated seeds last longer in storage than hybrid seeds. Variations in keeping quality are greater between species than between varieties of the same species.

To see if your seed is worth planting, you can dump some into a glass of water. Any that float are not viable. If you put in 10 seeds and seven float, your percentage is pretty low. Or you can germinate a few on a damp paper towel in a plastic sandwich bag. Don't let them dry out.

Also, watch to see if any of the seeds get moldy. As long as seed is alive, it will not mold because of a natural mold inhibitor.

If your seed is old and has a low percentage of viability, just planting the seeds thicker is probably not the answer. The old seeds may not produce plants that are as healthy.

The times seeds can be saved vary from one plant to another. Vegetables are easiest to save. Onion seeds can be saved one year, peas five years. Some flowers have well-known rules for length of viability, but by and large, most do not save well past one year.

No seed lasts forever. Although you have probably heard about wheat from the pyramids growing after centuries, there is no documentation of garden seeds lasting longer than 50 years. The Seed-Savers Exchange in Iowa has a network of people who plant things out to keep a supply of viable seed.

We tend to think of seeds as non-living things, but all kinds of changes are going on in seed during dormancy, even when it is not germinating. A seed is alive and breathing and, if it's not, it's dead. Even though seed may be alive, if it is very old, it may not be as healthy.

Seeds you collect in your garden must be allowed to dry before storage. Give them at least two weeks at room temperature, uncovered, to be sure they are dry.

Do I have to do anything special to my perennials as winter approaches?

There are three things your perennials will appreciate — just remember "deadhead," "mulch" and "water."
Perennials are plants that are going to live for more than a couple of years. Trees and shrubs are perennials, but they make wood. We'll be talking here mainly about herbaceous perennials — the plants that die back to the ground, but whose roots live and put up new stems and leaves in the spring.

Deadheading is simply cutting the plant back to within two or three inches of the ground. It doesn't matter when you do this — just cut them down when they start to look ugly. The important thing is that you not have dead plants left for pests and diseases to winter in. A bunch of dead leaves is an open invitation for those things.

When you are cutting off the tops is the time to check perennials for possible division. If you find that a plant is growing in a doughnut shape — stems in a circle with an empty space in the middle — you'll want to dig and divide it, probably next spring.

Mulch any new perennial its first winter and any marginal plant you hope will overwinter but aren't too sure about. Mulch at the time the ground freezes. If you're not sure when that is, Thanksgiving is usually a safe time.

Mulching is vital for first-year perennials because they haven't had a chance to develop good root systems yet. After two or three years they have deep roots that support them, even if the surface roots succumb to drought.

You can mulch with many kinds of organic stuff — pine needles, branches of any conifer and straw are possibilities. You want something open and loose that won't blow away. You are not trying to keep the plants warm; you are trying to keep them frozen.

If, when you bought a plant, it was labeled as hardy to

Zone 5, it is safer to mulch it even after the first year, unless you live in a protected area or in a town.

Many plants that die in winter die of drought, and mulching will help conserve moisture around the roots. Which brings us to watering.

It is important to send your perennials into winter with moist soil, so until the ground is frozen solid, you may want to give some things another drink.

This is most important with newly planted trees and shrubs because they don't yet have a well-developed root system. Give them a good, deep watering. There is not much danger of overwatering, but you don't want them to start growing again. You want them to keep progressing into dormancy and not to back out of it again.

It is recommended that trees and shrubs be moisture-stressed slightly as they go into dormancy, but if the fall weather is dry, they may well be stressed too much. An arctic blast could make them turn up their toes — or whatever dead trees turn up.

Spring bulbs should be damp and if you have beds with perennials that have dried out, water them, too. Just stick your fingers into the soil and if it is dry more than an inch down, add water.

If you had only native plants, they would be used to our harsh weather conditions, but here we are trying to grow all this other stuff that is really better-suited elsewhere.

Once the ground is frozen, you don't have to worry until you have a warm spell.

One recent winter was deadly for many perennials because in February we had two weeks with sunshine and warm temperatures every day. The plants were fooled into thinking it was spring and broke dormancy, only to be zapped later by sub-zero temperatures. And when a plant tries to break dormancy, it will die unless its roots have contact with available moisture.

An article in "Avant Gardener" also explains why it is important for your perennials and bulbs to go into the winter with damp soil. In the process of freezing, a molecule of water gives off heat, so in damp soil, the moisture acts as an insulating layer around plant roots.

You have probably heard that the reason for mulching your perennials is to prevent them from being heaved out of the ground by the frost. Actually, Montanans are not likely to find their delphinium shot out of the soil and lying on top of the ground, but it doesn't take anything that drastic to cause damage. All it takes is enough heaving to tear some of the plant's roots.

General pruning of trees and shrubs comes in late winter, but if you have maple, birch or walnut trees that need to be pruned, it must be done before the end of November. These trees have the root pressure that allows maples to be tapped for sugar; if you wait until spring, the sap will leak.

Winter

CONTINUED NEXT PAGE

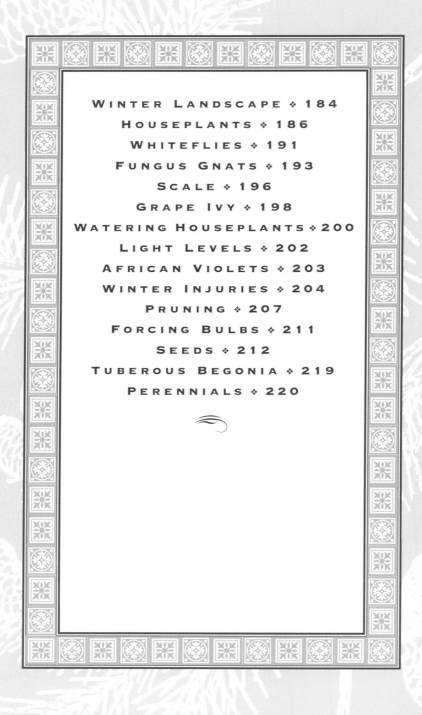

My Christmas cactus just won't bloom; what could be its problem?

 My big, old Christmas cactus used to bloom really well. It still looks healthy, but it doesn't bloom as much as it used to. What can I do for it?

 Last year my Christmas cactus made buds just after Thanksgiving. Then I brought it out where I could look at it and the buds all dried up. How can I keep that from happening again?

 The answer to all of these questions is probably the same single word — light. There are short-day plants, long-day plants and plants that could not care less. Christmas cactus is a short-day plant. When it gets a lot of light, it thinks it's the season to make leaves, which it does, forgetting all about flowering. That's why the plants bloom in the winter when the days are short.

If it was growing outside (and didn't die, as it would here) it would take care of itself and bloom when the days were the right length. But when it lives indoors where you turn on the lights after sunset, it is fooled into thinking it's a long day and makes leaves instead of flowers.

It needn't be in total darkness, but it requires dim light to set buds.

If it resides in a room the family keeps brightly lit in the evening, you could move it to an unlit room, or at least turn off lights that are near it.

If you keep the cactus a long way from the light source, it may think it's twilight, which doesn't count. But if you can sit by the plant and read, it's getting too much light. You may not have to move the plant if you can keep its part of the room dim. Don't turn on a light within about 10 feet of it.

If you are going to move the plant to a darker location or cut down on the artificial light that reaches it, you need to start in early winter. The buds develop very slowly and you won't see any for at least a month—perhaps even two.

People have all sorts of regimens to make their Christmas cacti bloom. Some move them to a back bedroom, others let them dry out and others keep them extra cool. If you do that and your cactus is blooming nicely, keep on doing that. But if it needs fixing, start by analyzing and adjusting its light.

The big, old cactus may have stopped blooming because of a change in its light situation, but it also could need pruning. While some cultivars do very well as large plants, others fare much better when kept pruned.

Don't prune now, of course, when you want buds to develop. The best time is just after the plant blooms. You can cut it back as far as you want to. Anything that looks shapely is all right.

There are several slightly different forms of Christmas cacti. Some used to be called *Zygocactus*, but now they are all lumped together in the genus *Schlumbergera*, after a 19th-century Belgian horticulturist named Frederick Schlumberger.

They have been extensively hybridized and there are many nice cultivars bred for unusual color, size and number of blooms, and the lasting quality of the flowers.

Sometimes Christmas cacti will bloom again in the spring when the day length is the same as their fall bud-developing season, although the bloom may not be as profuse.

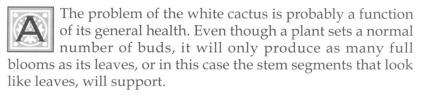

My two Christmas cactus plants live under exactly the same conditions and both set plenty of buds, but the red one gets lots of blossoms and about half the buds of the white one turn brown and never open.

The problem of the white cactus is probably a function of its general health. Even though a plant sets a normal number of buds, it will only produce as many full blooms as its leaves, or in this case the stem segments that look like leaves, will support.

Can I keep the bulbs I plan to force in my cold frame? I saw that done on a TV program.

 Not unless you have a way to keep them from getting warm, and we don't know how that could be done in this climate of variable temperatures. If the bulbs have started growing roots, it takes only a day or so of warm weather to get them started growing leaves and buds.

 I am tempted to buy one of the amaryllis bulbs that are so nice and cheap now. Will it grow and bloom? Do I just follow the directions on the package?

 The answers to your questions are yes, and yes, and no. There is nothing wrong with the inexpensive amaryllis bulbs, although you may occasionally get a bad one. If you just want to grow your bulb, enjoy its blooms and throw it away, do follow the instructions on the box. If you want to keep it and bring it into bloom again next winter, you have to follow a little different regimen.

The more expensive bulbs may be larger, but are most likely to be just new varieties or colors. All amaryllis are *Hippeastrum* from the Greek, meaning "horse star," because their blossoms are large and star-shaped. They came originally from South America, which is why they bloom in winter here in the Northern Hemisphere. They have been so hybridized and crossbred that nobody knows anymore exactly what species most of them are.

Amaryllis grow prodigious root systems—long, thick, brittle ones—which are trimmed off so the bulbs can be shipped. A new bulb will grow and bloom just from the nutrients stored in it. But if you want to save it from year to year, you need to see to it that it grows a healthy new root system—and then don't trim those roots off. Amaryllis are a long-lived bulb that can last up to 25 years if properly cared for.

If you buy a bulb planted in a plastic pot without drainage holes, melt some holes in the bottom with a heated nail or screwdriver.

Even if you only plan to keep your amaryllis one season, it is a good idea to throw away the peat or fiber it comes planted in and re-pot it in good potting soil. You will be rewarded with bigger and better flowers. Put the peat in the compost bin or mix some of it in with your potting soil. Amaryllis in straight peat are like narcissus in a bed of rocks — they do better in a more nutritive medium.

Don't bury the bulb. Keep a quarter to half of the bulb up out of the soil. Amaryllis need crowded conditions to thrive, so the pot should be only 1 inch larger, all the way around, than the bulb itself.

Probably the first thing you will see grow from a new bulb is a bloom stalk, but after saving a bulb over a season, you can't predict whether the first sprout will be a bloom or a leaf. It takes about five leaves for one bloom stalk. Each bloom stalk on a healthy bulb should produce four or five flowers, and the average is two bloom stalks per bulb. The leaves grow from the center of the bulb neck, while bloom stalks usually are produced off to the side.

Be prepared to stake your plant because it will almost surely be quite tall. The plant likes bright sun and cool temperatures. Give it at least half a day of sun until the first bud starts to open, then put it wherever you want to admire it. Clip off the flowers as they fade and trim the bloom stalk close to the bulb when the last blossom dies. Amaryllis should be kept moist, but not allowed to stand in a puddle.

To save the bulb for another year's bloom, give it plenty of light — a south or west window is best. It should grow more leaves — nine or 10 of them, 2-3 feet long. If you tie them up to a stake, you can keep the plant in a tall vase shape and prevent it from taking over your entire room.

In August, start to dry the bulb out by gradually reducing waterings over a few weeks until you stop watering it entirely. *do not* give it *any* water at all or it will not bloom again. Once a leaf turns yellow, cut it off. When all leaves are gone, just let it be dormant. It then needs four weeks of cool and dark conditions and four more weeks of warm and dark. Put it in the basement or crawl space first for its cool period, then move it to the coat closet or cupboard for its warm spell. Mark your calendar to remind you when it's time to move it. This is the time it sets buds — approximately October to December. At the end of the second four weeks, check to see if it has outgrown its pot, but if you re-pot it, do not trim or break off roots.

If you want to save the bulb, but don't want to keep it around the house all summer, you can put it outside after all danger of frost is past. Put it where it will get half a day of sun. Putting an amaryllis outside will change its cycle, however, more or less to the Northern Hemisphere. It will probably bloom right after you bring it inside in early fall. Just keep watering it as you have been and bring it indoors before frost — it won't tolerate a single degree of frost.

Your bulb may make little offsets. If it does, you can cut the little ones off once their leaves start getting in the way and pot them separately. It will take two to three years for offsets to bloom.

I bought and planted some amaryllis bulbs to give as Christmas gifts, but they are already growing too fast. Is there anything I can do to slow them down?

 If you had a greenhouse where you could control the temperature, humidity and day length exactly, you could read in a book just how long it would take from planting to bloom. However, when you are dealing with all the variables implicit in a home situation, you can only estimate about how long it might take. It's *very* "about."

There are some things you can do to put the brakes to your amaryllises. (Actually, we like to call them amarylli, but we aren't sure there is such a word.) We can only hope that these techniques will slow growth down enough to make the plants suitable gifts.

First, you can cut back a little on water. Just don't reduce it too much or the plant won't bloom at all.

Second, you can put the bulbs in a cooler place. You could move them to a cool, spare bedroom each night after sundown, for instance. Try to give them temperatures in the 60s rather than the 70s. As with water, don't lower the temperature too much.

Do not fertilize the plants.

Whatever else you do, do not cut down on light. It will only result in the bloom stalks' growing taller and more top-heavy.

If a plant starts to bloom before you give it, you can prolong the flower's life by picking off the six anthers as soon as the blossom opens. As the bud opens, the anthers look like inch-long caterpillars. If you can remove them before they have a chance to pollinate, you'll give the flower longer life.

Once the flowers open, take the plant out of the sun. Move it to the interior of the room, but watch it closely and turn it often—the plant is very phototropic and quickly bends toward the light, making it extremely susceptible to toppling.

As a last resort, you may be able to cut off the first spent bloom stalk. Your gift will produce a second one if your bulbs were pretty good ones to begin with.

In Elvin McDonald's "The New Houseplant" the author states that the original of our current amaryllis bulbs came not from South Africa, as previously believed, but from Peru. They have been bred in South Africa, Holland and the United States, but the species *dittatum*, from which our most common amaryllis varieties come, was South American.

Some of the more recent introductions are smaller-flowered and apparently started in Brazil.

McDonald says the smaller ones tend to be more evergreen than the standard, large-flowered varieties. Apparently they don't need to have their foliage dry out completely to recharge for the next blooming season.

Molly agrees. Her "Scarlet Baby" sat without water for two months before she finally cut the last of the green leaves off. So, as long as you give them at least two months of complete dry, don't worry about the leaves not turning brown. Current information is that you should not cut off the old leaves. Begin watering the plant again, and let it decide how it feels about mixing the new and the old.

Just before Christmas is a very good time to buy amaryllis bulbs. In order to get a specific color, you might have to pay a premium price, but just because the bulbs are inexpensive does not mean they will not produce a lovely plant with beautiful flowers.

The reason that some bulbs are so cheap is usually that the variety (like the red "Minerva" or pink-and-white "Apple Blossom") is particularly easy to grow, produces more offsets and is healthy, all around.

If you want to impress the socks off somebody without any effort, talent or know-how, buy three cheap amaryllis bulbs, put them all in one 8-inch pot full of potting soil and start watering them. This will make one really gorgeous gift. You could put them in a rusty old bucket and the recipient would never even notice the container.

If you have any leftovers—post-bloom amaryllis bulbs

you haven't let dry out—don't despair. Dry them out starting now. Gradually cut down their moisture over two or three weeks. They still need two months of dryness—three won't hurt. Put the pot in a cool, dark place—down in the basement or on the floor at the back of a closet.

Just remember they are there. One acquaintance was horrified to discover the amaryllis she had left in the dark months ago was six inches high and almost pure white.

They won't bloom for the holidays, of course, but they will flower in the spring.

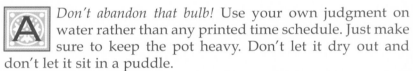 I saved my last year's amaryllis and am now starting it again. The directions say to water it once a week, but it gets so dry between waterings. It is OK to water it more often? Also, it is putting up leaves, but I see no sign of a flower bud. Should I just give up on this plant and start over?

Don't abandon that bulb! Use your own judgment on water rather than any printed time schedule. Just make sure to keep the pot heavy. Don't let it dry out and don't let it sit in a puddle.

Be patient and your amaryllis will probably put up a blossom from a different layer of the bulb. When a plant is healthy, you are likely to get leaves first. A new bulb often puts up a bloom first or at the same time as its leaves, either because its roots had been cut off before shipping or because of conditions under which it was stored.

Georgianna kept her first Christmas amaryllis and revived it when the next year's bulb finished blooming. She enjoyed gorgeous flowers even larger than the ones it produced its first winter. Her leaves were almost a foot high before the flower bud emerged from an outer layer of the bulb.

My amaryllis blossoms have faded. I want to save the bulb. Do I cut off the bloom stalk?

 Yes. Remove the old flower stem, and only that. The leaves must be left attached until they turn brown and keel over.

If you pinch the bulb and it feels spongy, don't worry. When you leave the leaves on, with the help of sunlight and chlorophyll, you get a miracle. Blooey! Photosynthesis fills the bulb with energy and gets it ready for another season.

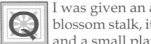 I was given an amaryllis saved from last year. It has no blossom stalk, its leaves are spreading all over the place, and a small plant seems to be growing next to the large one. What on earth do I do with it?

 Just tie all the leaves together loosely with string or yarn near the base to keep the plant in a nice, vase shape. Eventually you may need to stake it — the less sun it gets, the longer the leaves and flower stalks get.

An amaryllis has a very nice shape if tied up at reasonable intervals.

Even if your plant has had leaves for three weeks, that doesn't mean it won't make a flower stalk. The plants do things at their own individual rates.

The baby plant on the side is an offset. You may leave it or cut it off from the big bulb. If you cut it off, you can relegate it to the compost bucket or remove it very carefully and try to get it to root and make a new plant. If it does grow, it won't bloom its first year or two. In fact, it could take as long as seven years to blossom.

Someone always sends me a blooming plant for Christmas. What can I do to keep it in bloom as long as possible? Can these greenhouse plants be kept as houseplants and brought into bloom again?

 Care, naturally, depends on the variety of plant. Poinsettias are the traditional Christmas flower and the most common, but according to local florists, azaleas, Christmas cactus and cyclamen are also popular. These are all things that provide color and are eager to bloom at this time of year.

Christmas cactus is not a desert cactus, but an understory jungle plant that thrives in wet, shady conditions. If you are given a Christmas cactus in full bloom, you can expect it to go downhill from there. It probably won't bloom again until next fall.

Azaleas want cool, damp conditions and are really an unhappy sort of plant. Keep them in the coolest part of the house with north or east exposure and temperatures in the 60s, if possible. Azaleas love Seattle. Do your best to give them Seattle in the middle of a Montana winter.

There is always a chance that your azalea will like your house, but it may decline after a month or so. If it does, don't blame yourself.

The spent flowers must be removed, because azaleas like to set seed, which inhibits continued bloom. You may be able to keep it going and it may bloom more than once in a year. If you don't want the grief, enjoy it and compost it after blooming.

Poinsettias, on the other hand, are from Mexico. They were introduced in this country by Joel Poinsett, U.S. ambassador to Mexico, in the late 1800s. Every plant you see now comes from one single plant, a mutant from a plant Poinsett found.

The problem with poinsettias is that they really want to grow into 7-foot hedges. They have to be cut back drastically. What you buy (or are given) is a cutting that may not be very well-rooted. It is likely to be fairly new, forced into bloom. Greenhouse conditions can control the time of bloom and, under good conditions, the plant can stay in bloom for two or even three months.

Poinsettias are really quite easy to care for. If it has foil or plastic around its pot when you receive it, make sure it has drainage. The plant will drink a lot and wants a fairly sunny location. If it gets bugs, it is hard to deal with because poinsettias don't like to be sprayed with anything.

Chrysanthemums seem destined to be loved and left. Florists like them because they can be forced into bloom any time of the year. It takes a lot to get them to re-bloom and between bloomings they're not that lovely. After it finishes blooming, take your mum tenderly to the compost pile and promise it that next year it can come back as paperwhites or as a poinsettia.

....

Many non-gardeners will have received plants as Christmas gifts from well-intentioned friends and relatives. If you find yourself in this position, what can you do to keep the plant alive until your mother's birthday, when you can give it to her?

The very first thing to do is to remove or punch holes in the plastic or foil that is almost always wrapped around the pot. Place a saucer under the pot.

If it has flowers, place it in a window.

If it has no flowers, you can place it somewhere within about 6 feet of a window, but not necessarily on a window sill.

Give the plant enough water that some shows up in the saucer. Set the timer for 10 minutes, then pour off all the water from the saucer.

Because different plants have different levels of thirst, it is impossible to say exactly how often you need to water. The best way is to walk by the plant every day and pick up the pot. When you notice that it is appreciably lighter weight, water it.

In case you are at someone's house and they present you with a plant, here are some extra rules for transporting it home:

If the temperature is below 40 degrees, put the plant in

a plastic bag. If it is below 20 degrees, double-bag it or put it in a box and put that in a plastic bag. Warm up the car before bringing out the plant. If you are walking home, tell the giver you'll drive by tomorrow and pick it up.

 The beautiful hibiscus I have had since last spring is losing leaves. They get yellow blotches that keep getting bigger until the whole leaf is yellow. This seems to be happening more and more. What's wrong?

 There may well be nothing wrong. We have just hit the time of year when days are too short. Hibiscus is native to areas where it never gets this cold and dark. It is originally from China and is common outdoors throughout the tropic zone.

However, the first thing you must do is make sure it doesn't have any bugs—especially sucking insects. If it is pest-free, work on its environment. If it is not in the sunniest part of the house, move it there. It would love a sunny window.

It also is possible that your hibiscus is deficient in some mineral, most likely a trace element. Check whatever fertilizer you give it to be sure it contains more than the standard nitrogen, phosphorus and potash. If the label doesn't list minerals like manganese and iron, use another one that does. Look for something organic like compost or seaweed derivatives as a source of trace minerals.

I'm worried about my hibiscus. Many leaves are yellowing and dropping, and the leaves have sticky spots on the back. There are a few webs where the leaves join the stems, but not many. Any ideas?

It sounds like mites and not much more. Some increase in yellowing is natural at this time of year. The sticky spots may also be natural. There is a process called water of guttation by which a plant evens up root pressure when all its tissues get wet. It expels the excess moisture through the leaves. The situation is fairly common in plants — like hibiscus — that require a lot of water, especially when they receive a big shot all at once.

Molly and Georgianna both have this sticky stuff on our hibiscus plants, but only notice it when looking for bugs. We may be wrong about its being water of guttation, which usually drips from leaf tips; ours has appeared at the bases of leaves.

Hibiscus leaves are not very long-lived and some yellowing of leaves is to be expected. The plants also go through periods when they drop an alarming number of leaves every day. Both of ours have gone through a period of this, although not at exactly the same time.

The growth pattern of hibiscus seems to be that a lot of leaves die off, a lot of new leaves sprout, the plant blooms, the baby leaves grow large and then the whole process starts again. There also is a definite connection between winter's low-light conditions and the heavy leaf drop.

If the plant does, indeed, have mites, it means that it is not a happy hibiscus. It is almost surely too hot, too dry, or both. You don't get mites on plants that are cool and damp. This is a very hazardous time of the year for producing the warm, dry conditions that mites love. When the furnace first comes on in the fall, there is still moisture in the house, but by now everything has pretty much dried out.

The solution may be to get a whole lot more plants to provide a bunch more evaporative and transpirative moisture. If that's not a practical solution, take a look at where your hibiscus is in relation to registers or other heat sources. The worst possible scenario is to have warmed, dry air circulating near it.

Once you figure out what the problem is, make corrections, then apply first aid in the form of water. Grab up an old Windex or 409 spray bottle, fill it with warm water and spritz the whole plant, concentrating on the sites of the webs and the backs of leaves. Do this every day for a week. It will not kill the mites, but it will make them want to move elsewhere. They will go and eat dust bunnies or live in the rug instead of sucking on your hibiscus.

We set a humidifier directly under a big, old hibiscus when mite webs first showed up and the plant has been obviously grateful for the cool moisture, and there have been no new webs.

If you change the plant's location and/or conditions and still get new webs, try spraying it twice a week with insecticidal soap for a few weeks. This should get rid of the mites, but if you haven't changed its environment to suit its needs, mites will return ere long.

....

he 4-foot hibiscus plant Georgianna adopted, when it began to crowd Molly out of her own living room, eventually had to be pruned. It was a traumatic experience for the adoptive parent.

Molly consented to be present at the surgery and to give advice, but she refused to wield the shears — she said Georgianna had to do it herself so the next time she wouldn't be afraid of the task.

"Cut off any branch that looks too long," she said. "Make a straight cut a quarter inch toward the branch tip from a leaf where new growth is showing. Don't trim more than a third of the branches at any one time. Trim some, then wait a week or two.

"Remember that wherever you prune, the limb is going to branch, so don't think about how the plant will look as soon as you finish—imagine how it will look when it puts on its new growth."

The first few cuts were painful for the surgeon, but after that they became successively easier. Her guilt was mitigated by the fact that she could trim up most of the clippings and put them in sterile potting soil to root, so now there is a veritable forest of hopeful-looking hibiscus trimmings in pots inside a dry cleaner's bag in a warm, light spot.

Molly warned that half of the cuttings could be expected to die, but if half of them live, Georgianna should be able to supply most of the state with double-pink hibiscus plants.

In the department of happy endings, amputee hibiscus responded exuberantly to its pruning. Within two weeks it was leafing out in all directions.

 My daughter sent me a gardenia for my birthday. It arrived in beautiful condition, but every time a bud looks like it might open the next day, it falls off instead. Is there anything I can do?

There may be nothing that will help. Gardenias are extremely temperamental and any time something displeases them, they announce their displeasure by dropping a bud. And they are very easily displeased. They are very picky plants.

Unfortunately, a house in Montana in midwinter doesn't normally have any of the things gardenias are picky about.

On the other hand, it may be that your gardenia just is not getting enough light. Temperature fluctuations also may cause bud drop. The plants like a cool, wet climate with lots of light and very acid soil. Your gardenia probably was potted in acid soil, but the water it has been getting is not acid.

Perhaps moving the plant to a sunnier location will help. Keep it away from hot, dry conditions. You may find if you do these things it will start to bloom in a month or so. If not, be patient a little longer. Spring and fall provide conditions gardenias like.

 I read your article on the gardenia that kept dropping its buds, but what if you can't even get it to bud? I received a small plant two years ago as a gift. It had some buds on at the time that never actually opened and has not bloomed since. The plant is now quite large and seems to be doing well, but I would like to know what I need to do to get it to bloom. I keep it where it gets plenty of light and try to water it often. A friend says she waters hers daily. Do you think it is my soil? If so, what do I do?

 Congratulate yourself on keeping alive a plant as difficult as a gardenia. They are native to the warmer areas of Asia and Africa and everything is wrong about trying to grow them as a houseplant in Montana.

There are many varieties, which used to be considered different species, but all now are classified as *jasminoides*. A plant bought from a florist may be one not planned for a long-term, re-blooming house plant. It might have been bred for the florist to force into bloom, producing a whole lot of blossoms, but very difficult to convince to bloom again.

Most gardenias tend to bloom in spring and summer, and any gardenia must have at least four hours of sun to set buds. The more sun they get, the more buds they'll produce at one time.

Because gardenias are picky in the extreme, they may want direct sun in a south window in the winter and by summer need to have their light filtered, depending on whether we are having a hot, dry spell or a cloudy spell.

They also need a fair amount of fertilizer, but not one high in nitrogen. If your fertilizer says 10-10-10, change to one with a second number considerably larger than the first—more phosphorus and less nitrogen.

Lack of iron is probably not your problem, as it would cause the leaves to turn yellow with dark green veins. Like azaleas, rhododendrons and holly, gardenias need acid soil. In an area like ours, the water can be alkaline enough to raise the pH level. To prevent this, you could include a lot of peat moss in the potting soil, feed it with fertilizer meant for acid-loving plants or buy it some iron sulfate.

Temperature is the trickiest thing with gardenias. They are happy with temperatures you like around the house in the daytime if you're not wearing two sweaters. However, if the thermometer falls below 60 degrees at night, they get a severe case of the sulks. If the night temperature climbs above 65 even once, any incipient bud forming will stop and the cycle must start over. If you have a wood stove, don't try to grow gardenias (or any other crotchety houseplants).

 I bought a lovely cyclamen at the grocery store and just a week later it's dying. What did I do wrong?

 Maybe nothing. A week is very early for a plant to die. It may have had something terminal when you got it.

As basic care, cyclamens like it cool, with good light, but not direct sun. They prefer to be kept moist, but not soggy. Don't let your plant dry out or its flower buds will drop off. If it gets soggy, it is likely to rot.

If you are the "I water my plants once a month whether they need it or not" type, you should probably not adopt a cyclamen. If you like to talk to your plants every day, you will check it often enough.

Four or five years is a pretty good length of time to keep one happy. Many people buy them as a Christmas plant and then compost them when they finish blooming.

Molly has had hers about four years. It hangs a foot or so inside a north window. When it stops blooming in summer, it goes outside on the north side of the house while it goes through a dormant period. It gets fewer, smaller leaves. When the weather gets cool, after it's been outside for about two months, it goes back inside. By the end of summer it has new leaves. After it comes inside it blooms within a month.

When you buy a cyclamen in bloom, look for buds, not just flowers that are open. Don't buy a plant that has no un-opened buds—it may have been mistreated or may be diseased. If leaves are puckered and funny-looking, it may have cyclamen mites.

Check the base of the stems and under the leaves and don't buy one with signs of mold or rot—it has been kept too wet.

As with any potted plant, heft the pot and don't buy one that is light weight. It has probably been allowed to dry out, and its buds will just fall off. Supermarkets don't necessarily take awfully good care of plants.

Be careful about getting a cyclamen cold. Ask the clerk to double wrap the plant. Have the car on and the heater going before you take the plant out, or wait until a warmer day to buy it.

 How can I keep the deer out of my flower beds and vegetable garden?

 This is one of the most frequently asked questions we get. We wish there were a simple, direct answer, but there just isn't. If there were, there wouldn't be so many troubled gardeners.

The surest methods are a really good fence or a big, loud dog that sleeps outside at night. We don't have a minimum height to recommend for the dog, but the fence needs to be at least 6 feet high. An electric fence is effective and can be just a single strand 3 feet off the ground. A local nursery has had very good luck protecting their stock with a 6-foot, high-tech electric fence most home gardeners wouldn't care to finance. Perhaps there is a happy medium somewhere.

Molly built a 6-foot wire fence that has kept out every-thing but an aggressive moose that bent the foot-traffic gate and an athletic deer that high-jumped it. Her drive-through gate is monitored by a motion sensor that turns on a bright spotlight and emits a high beep. If deer visit your yard only at night, you would need only the light.

If you don't want a 6-foot fence, you can erect two 3-foot fences not more than 5 feet apart. The deer cannot jump both fences at one time, and the narrow space between fences pre-vents them from taking off again if they land between.

Fences are a long-term solution, but a major expense. There are several repellent sprays and a myriad of home reme-dies designed to keep the deer out of your lettuce and lychnis.

Ropel is the only spray we have found that doesn't wash off. The plants incorporate it into their systems and it lasts about six months. However, you will have to spray several times in the spring as new leaves and then flower buds appear.

Ropel contains one of the most bitter substances known to man and it makes the plants taste very bad, so be sure not to get it on any food plant—it doesn't taste any better to people than it does to deer.

It is important to spray before deer have begun brows-ing your garden. It is much easier to keep them from starting than to make them quit eating your plants. Deer are creatures of habit—they keep on doing what they have been doing and keep eating what they have been eating. If they taste your peony sprouts and find them delicious before you spray, they will prob-ably keep on tasting one after another after you spray, looking for one that doesn't taste bitter.

If you have just one or a few trees, like the ornamental crabs and mountain ash the deer find particularly delectable, it will pay you to put a fence around them high enough that the deer can't reach over it. One deer can do a lot of damage to a tree just taking one bite a night, checking to see if it has recovered from its bitterness.

We planted a bulb bed in our churchyard and sprayed the tulips with Ropel. Out of 100 tulips in the bed, the deer nibbled only about three plants at each end of the area before giving up and dining elsewhere. The next year they apparently remembered that those were bad-tasting tulips. They didn't sample the plants at all.

R opel also is effective for mice and voles. If you spray a band around the perimeter of a greenhouse or cold frame, the little critters will rarely cross it.
Ropel is not cheap, but a quart will protect the average yard from deer for a year. After the first year's use, you shouldn't have to spray as much.

We also have used a repellent called Hinder, which is a concoction mixed to smell like bear urine. It is effective, but it lasts only three to four weeks and washes off, so you can't use it in rainy weather or if you use sprinkler irrigation, unless you cover the sprayed plants first.

The American Rose Society used Hinder by putting the substance in cutoff milk cartons and covering them with lattice to keep out the rain.

Manure from the cat houses of zoos is sold as a repellent, but unless you have a zoo nearby, that hardly seems like a reasonable solution.

The old standby Forest Service remedy is a mixture of two raw eggs beaten into a gallon of water and sprayed on plants. Deer don't like the odor, but it doesn't smell bad when stored in your refrigerator, you don't notice the smell in the garden and it washes off, so you can use it on vegetables.

A careful study in an orchard showed that bars of soap hung in trees cut deer damage by 70 percent within 3 feet of the soap, but had absolutely no effect past that distance. The soap brand made no difference to the animals, but at 3-foot intervals, several trees would take a pretty impressive number of bars.

Hair clippings collected from your hairdresser or dog

groomer, tied in a section of pantyhose and placed 10 feet apart around the perimeter of the garden work for a while, too.

Cornell University did an experiment with Milorganite, an organic fertilizer containing such goodies as sewage and brewery waste. The product was applied at a rate of five pounds per 100 square feet in an area with about 40 deer per square mile. It was reapplied one or two times a month and after every snowfall. The deer stayed away, but the experiment is continuing to see for how long it works.

That's the trouble with repellents — they only work for so long before the deer get used to them and begin counting them as the price they must pay for spinach sprouts and begonia buds.

Of course, you can decide to plant only things deer don't like, but you should realize that your list will be very short. You can try planting the things deer avoid around the edge of your garden and their favorites in the center, but the deer don't seem to mind wading through the Oriental poppies and rudbeckia to get to the roses and delphinium.

Two ideas on discouraging deer from devouring your Double Delight roses have come from a Spokane rose nursery. They have found that deer do not eat their Alba roses. Albas are old-fashioned shrub roses with a short blooming season. They include such varieties as Blush Hip, Queen of Denmark and Maiden's Blush.

The nursery also has discovered that criss-crossing 30-pound-test monofilament fishing line through rose bushes makes it a pain in the neck to work with the plants, but it also deters the deer. We can tell you from experience that a single strand of fish line does not work.

After a big post-Christmas snow, the deer started eating my junipers and have stripped them of every trace of green except a tuft at the tip that they can't reach. Will the poor things recover? And if they do, how can I prevent the same thing from happening again next year?

The junipers will probably come back, but now that the deer have discovered your junipers, they have undoubtedly put them on their list of regular stops. They will keep checking them out, so you need to start now to protect what you have left.

You can cover the shrubs with chicken wire or bird netting or criss-cross enough nylon fishing line around them to keep deer muzzles out. You could put fences around them. You could spray them with Ropel, although that would be fairly expensive if you have many junipers.

You could put up a simple electric fence—string a hot wire and plug it in at night, when most deer damage occurs. Just don't forget to unplug it in the morning or you may end up zapping your neighbor.

You can try some of the short-term cures that might work until the deer leave. Hang bags of hair no more than 5 feet apart, use egg spray, string fishing line 6 inches apart on poles. Stake your dog out there.

An item in "Avant Gardener" claimed that hanging fabric softener sheets 10 feet apart kept deer away for up to eight weeks. You wouldn't want to use the unscented ones—it's probably the smell that repels the deer.

The junipers will almost surely grow back, but it may not be right away and it may not be all over at once. They might start right away or they might take all summer, so don't get discouraged and dig them out.

Also, just because only parts of the bush turn green, it doesn't necessarily mean that the rest won't join in later. Try to be patient. The ugliness isn't terminal.

Your yard is not the only place with deer problems. We

have read of three arboretums that have employed unusual means of controlling deer damage.

The Shaw Arboretum in St. Louis conducted a lottery in which 150 hunters won the right to hunt on the grounds — with muzzle loaders only.

The University of Wisconsin at Madison had a deer population of 60 on just 2 square miles. Not only was the facility losing trees, but it was getting unnatural forest regrowth in the wake of the deer damage. They called in sharpshooters from the state to reduce the population to 10 animals.

Morris Arboretum at the University of Pennsylvania put its rose garden in the paws of Morris, a Jack Russell terrier.

The little deer-chasing breed was developed in England for hunters to carry in their coats and set loose when game was sighted. The rose garden remained deer-free after Morris' arrival, for almost a year. Then Morris had to be retired and retrained as a house dog. It seems his bark was much worse than his bite. In fact, he was all bark and no bite. Being no fools, the deer eventually figured this out and stopped running away from him. Drat! Another promising deer repellent down the drain.

A Pennsylvania man with an acreage of natural woods stapled bird netting to the trees on the perimeter of the whole plot to protect it from marauding wildlife. He was looking for something that would keep the deer out and wouldn't look ugly. The bird netting, he reported, works fine and is all but invisible. Sounds like a lot of bird netting.

 My new poinsettia started dropping its lower leaves almost as soon as I brought it home. Can I do anything to save it?

 It almost certainly got too dry. This is typical behavior for a drought-stricken plant. Feel the dirt in the pot and don't buy a dry one, no matter how cheap it is. A poinsettia that has been allowed to dry out is going to drop its leaves, although it may be a week or two before you see the damage.

Water your plant well, keep it continually moist and give it light. It might be OK. Once it stops dropping leaves, you've got it made. Good luck.

 My gardens are so lovely in the summer and so ugly in winter. Is there anything short of a complete re-land-scaping that can make my yard easier to look at this time of year?

 Our frost-free season is only a quarter of the year. Fur-thermore, no matter how much you love a particular plant, it is probably only going to bloom for a two- or three-week period.

If you work very hard, choosing plants with varied blooming seasons from very early spring to very late fall, you may be able to extend your garden's blooming season to a max-imum of eight months.

So the winter answer is to think about things that do not bloom. Now is a good time to look critically at your garden, when its plants are bare and you can see its basic structure. Be-sides, you are trapped in the house anyway. Look at your gar-dens from all your windows and see how your homemade view looks. There are three primary principles to consider:

First, think about the perspectives from which the view will be seen. This is the angle from which an area should look best. Is it pretty now? Do you want to change something? The non-growing things assume added importance in the winter.

Most people prefer to lay out their gardens along either straight lines, which give a formal effect, or in curves, which are informal. As you look out at your garden, visualize how it might look if you added a curved path, a spreading trellis or cedar ar-bor. Next winter, would you like to see a fence corner, a bench or a bed raised by a double row of railroad ties? Then decide if the expense would be worth it.

The second consideration is trees — the biggest plants you have. It's nice to have some evergreens because they add winter color. However, using nothing but evergreens gives a dark effect. Look at your deciduous trees. When it gets warmer, could they be trimmed to give them better shapes?

Make notes now on where you may want to add a tree, thinking about how it will look as a baby next spring and what it will be like in five or 10 years. Many trees develop pretty bark as they age, which will add even more texture and contrast to your winter garden. Trees are very handy for covering up unsightly views, but you don't want to close out something that enhances your vista.

The third important component is shrubs, which give the garden its horizontal lines, as opposed to the vertical lines contributed by trees. They can be planted in clumps for a tree-like statement or in a line to form a boundary.

When choosing shrubs, consider their winter shapes and colors. Dogwoods and barberries add splashes of lovely red, while willows may be gold or orange.

Once you have contemplated the skeleton for your garden, think about filling in with flowers, grasses and so on. At least one clump of a grass like blue fescue, fountain grass or quaking grass may be called for. The dry leaves and seedstalks look nice and they reseed the grasses that are annuals.

Several trees, shrubs and ground covers produce attractive berries that perk up your garden — at least until the birds harvest them. Consider mountain ash, honeysuckle, Oregon grape, kinnikinnick, dogwood, viburnum, currants and flowering fruit trees.

You needn't cut off flowering plants as soon as frost kills them — many have a nice winter form. Just cut them down before the spring growth starts.

You are wise to think about these things now. In the spring you will be so busy planting that you won't have time to contemplate and you won't be able to assess your garden's structure once everything has leafed out.

185

My houseplants are not doing well. Some have died and the rest seem to be ailing. My 23-year-old angel-wing begonia has lots of leaves on the bottom, but the older ones don't look good. My aloe vera has white spots the size of pinheads—I think they are mold. What can be going on?

 It is probably not the same thing affecting all your plants. Houseplants just coming to the end of a long, tough time of low light and dry air need a little extra tender loving care. Be sure that you don't overwater in low-light conditions when the plants aren't growing as fast as usual. Give them a kick start into spring with a little dose of fertilizer.

Plants know it's spring. Even plants under lights that have the same number of footcandles of light every day can somehow tell. Plants that only have a once-a-year growth spurt start growing, whether we humans realize it's spring or not.

As for your begonia, a plant that old is a really OLD plant! Remember that no matter how much you love it, it is not going to live forever. Most plants that live a long time get stemmy. You could start a couple of cuttings and plant them in the same pot with the parent plant.

When you plant a seed to grow a new plant, it's like two people having a child. Cuttings, on the other hand, produce clones, so the new plants will actually be a continuation of the old one.

This is an opportune time for re-potting, and the begonia (or any of your other ailing houseplants) will not be upset if you take it out of its pot and check its roots. Have the dirt fairly wet but not soggy. With the base of the stem between your fingers, turn the pot over and lift it off the soil ball. A flexible plastic pot can be squeezed from opposite directions to loosen it, and the plant lifted out. If it doesn't come out easily, run a table knife around the edge of the pot to loosen the dirt from the pot.

If you find roots growing out of the drain hole(s), cut them off—they will die anyway. If you see more roots than dirt, the plant needs a new pot. If the main roots circle the pot, cut the circling ones off.

Plants are not animals and they act differently. They don't mind having their roots trimmed any more than you mind cutting your toenails. And, just as you can grow toenails, the plant can grow new roots.

Roots grow from the tips. If you leave the roots spiraling, they can't find their way into new soil. When you cut them, you make new tips and they will start growing out into the soil right away.

If the roots you see around the outside of the soil ball are only the small, fibrous ones, just give them more dirt to grow in.

We would be surprised if the little white, fuzzy spots on your aloe vera are mold, especially if they are all about the size of a pinhead. Mold does not come evenly sized and spaced. Aloe is a succulent and you have surely been keeping it fairly dry, so it is not likely to get mold anyway. Your spots are probably mealy bugs.

Dip a cotton swab in alcohol and touch it to each white spot. That's the recommended treatment for mealy bugs and works better than any potent pesticide. You do need to hang in and keep an eye on things—it's not a one-shot deal. Check them every day for a while, then file the situation in the back of your mind and check weekly. If the spots start reappearing, treat them again.

 I have inherited a crown of thorns that has not been touched in 20 years. It has long, bare stems with leaves only at the tips. It is a huge plant but in a little tiny pot. It has great sentimental value for me and I don't want to discard it, but what can I do to make it look better?

 Your first step is to prune the plant—ruthlessly. Cut it WAY back. What you see is the plant's natural form. It is a euphorbia, like the poinsettia, and if you met one in a southern California garden, it might be a bush 3 feet by 4 feet, consisting of almost nothing but bare stems. That's ugly by houseplant standards.

Fortunately, crown of thorns does not mind pruning in the least. Cut each stem back to 4 inches, or until it stops looking so repulsive. If a stem has branches, cut to 4 inches above the fork. It has a latex sap, so do your trimming over a drop cloth or layers of newspaper in case it drips.

This will get the plant back to a manageable size. Each place you cut, the plant will send one or two stems or branches out. Cover your bases by clipping 6-inch tips off some of your prunings, let the cut ends dry half an hour or so and try to root them in damp soil.

Once the plant has been severely pruned, it won't need as much water, so be careful not to drown it.

If it really hasn't been touched in 20 years, it also will have to be re-potted. It undoubtedly needs some new soil and would probably love some fertilizer. Don't do everything at once. Prune and fertilize it, then wait a couple of weeks before re-potting. It should breathe a sigh of relief and say, "Oh, thank you."

Give it a few weeks to get back on track. And if you get worried about your plant's heavy leaf drop, rest easy. Its leaves are very short-lived.

How do you know whether to fertilize houseplants in the winter? Some books say you should stop.

 Don't stop fertilizing everything. Some plants, like geraniums and fuchsia, want to go partially dormant and should not be fertilized. Others, like hibiscus, hoya and jasmine, bloom intermittently in winter and should receive some food. You can be sure that a plant like impatiens that wants to bloom needs some fertilizer, although in the shorter days of winter, it doesn't require as much. You might go to half strength while fertilizing on the same time schedule, giving it a continuous supply, but in smaller quantities.

There is no easy answer. Watch your plant and try to figure out what it is trying to do.

 I can grow almost anything outdoors, but when I come indoors, my green thumb turns brown. I give my houseplants plenty of water, but they die anyway. Does anybody else have this problem?

 Lots of people do, and the most common cause is overwatering. You may be killing your houseplants with kindness.

It is important to understand the differences in growing conditions in the garden and in a pot. Outdoors, a plant has unrestricted root room and its roots vary from half the size of the plant's top to three times the size of the top. An outdoor plant may have from 2-50 feet of drainage.

In a container, a plant has root space much smaller than its top and only 3-10 inches of drainage—just the depth of its pot.

Of course plants do need water, which they take in through their roots, but they also must get air. If they can't get it, they die. In the garden, they get air to their roots all the time because the water drains away well and there is air between the soil particles. With cramped root spaces, your plants need all the air they can get, so be careful not to fill air space with water.

In a container, you must provide access to air for your plant's roots. The two most important ways are to provide drainage and to take care in the choice of potting mixtures.

Except for a few plants, like papyrus and umbrella plants which are native to swamps, plants do not like to have wet feet. Plants need a pot with holes in the bottom, set on a saucer. Soil can get quite dense after a while and water permeates it slowly, so check saucers 10-15 minutes after watering and if there's water, pour it off.

We used to be told to put pebbles in the bottom of the pot for drainage, but that is not necessary—the rocks just take up room that would be better occupied with soil.

Unless you have very sandy garden soil, don't use it for potting. Sandy loam is the best garden soil but in a pot it is lousy because it keeps packing down. You need to mix garden soil with things that will maintain open air spaces—perlite or sand, for instance. Perlite is a mineral expanded by heat and is very lightweight. It does float, however, and hence must be stirred back into the soil again occasionally. If you use sand, buy a good grade of coarse sand, also called builder's sand. Kitty litter does not work because it dissolves.

If you buy your potting soil, get the best you can find, which usually means the most expensive. Cheap stuff may lack nutrients or water-holding capability, or both. If you have a choice between one that has some loam in it and one called "soilless mixture," buy the one with the loam. As good as we are at mixing dirt, we're not as good at it as God is yet.

If you decide to mix your own, you might try this recipe, which we find works for us. Combine a quart each of garden soil, perlite and peat moss. If you have compost, mix in three cups—plants love compost. To the mixture, add a tablespoon of dolomitic lime to counteract the acid in the peat moss. Compost is very high in nitrogen so if you use that, also add a tablespoon of superphosphate. (If you are an organic purist, you may add phosphate as bonemeal or rock phosphate.) If you do not have compost, stir in 2 tablespoons of a complete fertilizer.

Get used to hefting your houseplants' pots so you can tell by how light they feel that it's time to give them a drink. Plants making buds drink more than they do any other time, and plants need less water in the shorter winter days. Just because you know how to water a plant in April doesn't mean that schedule will do in November.

You can't avoid root rot by not introducing it into the house. The fungi that cause it are there all the time, but they don't hurt the plant as long as its roots are healthy.

Also, recent tests have borne out the advice your granny probably gave you—that it is better for plants to be watered with water at room temperature to lukewarm. The tests show that plants develop better root systems when watered with warm, rather than cold, water.

 I just can't seem to keep an ivy alive in the winter. Can my gas heat be affecting them?

 Yes, your heating system could have killed your ivy. Many houseplants do not tolerate gas heat. Ivy is one of them. No matter how efficient a gas furnace is, there are always unburned particles in the air. If your ivies thrive when it's not the heating season, this is one of the things to suspect if the plants sicken once the furnace comes on in the fall.

 I had whiteflies on the tomato plants in my green-house, but once the tomatoes were gone and I was growing lettuce, I didn't see any more.
One place I asked about them told me to wash down the walls with bleach. Now I am ready to put in some new tomatoes. Is it safe to assume the whiteflies are gone for good?

What a beautiful dream! Unfortunately, you are quite likely to wake up to a new infestation of whiteflies.

They love tomatoes and don't like lettuce, and wiping the walls with bleach is unlikely to have any effect whatsoever on their population.

The common whitefly, which is the kind we are likely to get here, is not a problem outdoors because it cannot overwinter in our climate.

However, it can be a major pest in houseplants or greenhouses because its favorite temperature range, just like ours, is 65-75 degrees. That is the range in which it is most comfy, lays the most eggs and has the best survival rate.

The Latin name of common whiteflies is *Trialeurodes vaporariorum*, which means something like "they appear out of thin air." They don't, of course, but they can reproduce either sexually or asexually. All you need is one female and you are in business. One mama can lay 200-400 eggs without benefit of a daddy.

The eggs are all but invisible. The creatures go through four larval stages. The first is the crawler stage, the only time they move. They are a dirty-white and slightly translucent. They go through three more stages, never moving, before they pupate.

You don't have to wonder if what you see is whiteflies. No other insect looks anything like them. The adult is snowy white and looks triangular, rather than rounded. They flutter their wings very fast and fly a pretty much level course.

Prevention is your only salvation. If you have only a very few, you can squash them before daylight or after dark. For a minor infestation, sticky cards can be used, not to control them, but to let you know for sure whether you have them. You can buy them or make your own by coating a yellow card with Tanglefoot.

Insecticidal soap, horticultural oils and neem are all that has a prayer of controlling whiteflies because they have developed immunity to all known insecticides permitted for general use.

Even if you're not an organic gardener, don't drag out the

pesticides—you have to go organic to be effective. Though the package may say the product will kill whiteflies, if you can buy it, it almost certainly won't do the job.

If you have very many on any plant, no matter how much you love it, get it out of there! Before you buy a greenhouse plant, check the backs of leaves carefully and if you find even one whitefly, go somewhere else for your purchase.

It is possible to vacuum off whiteflies, which commercial greenhouses do sometimes. However, if you do this, you must freeze the vacuum cleaner bag for at least 24 hours to kill the bugs. For houseplants and home greenhouses, this is not the treatment of choice.

Food crops like tomatoes tolerate enough whiteflies to cover a third of the plant's leaf surface without affecting its yield. With ornamentals, it is worth trying to control whiteflies if you have fewer flies than the plant has leaves—otherwise, get rid of it.

If you decide that you can live with a few whiteflies, remember that you and the whiteflies may disagree on desirable population levels.

If you decide to treat a plant, be prepared for two to four weeks of checking the backs of the leaves under a strong light every single day. You really have to stay with the program. Don't stop until you haven't seen a single one for several days.

Eggs may hatch over a 30-day period. In fact, Molly thinks eggs may drop off leaves and lie dormant in the soil even longer than a month. If there is anything that will make you believe in spontaneous generation, the whitefly will do it.

 Help! Whenever I water my amaryllis a bunch of little gray bugs fly up. How can I get rid of them? Will they attack my other plants?

 Relax. Your little gray bugs are fungus gnats. Like the springtails you may see hopping in your plant saucer when you lift the pot or on top of the soil when you water, they cause little or no harm. Your plants don't mind their presence.

Fungus gnats and springtails are the "good bugs" of houseplant-dom. They live in potting soil where they recycle vegetable matter and seldom feed on the plant. Springtails never leave the pot.

Although they don't bother your plants, the fungus gnats may pose a threat to your own sanity if they get to be too numerous. If this happens, pour or spray a little half-strength insecticidal soap solution on the soil a couple of times until they're under control.

For those of you pestered by fungus gnats in your houseplants, good news. There is a special strain of *Bacillus thuringiensis*, Bt/H-14, which seems to provide effective control.

Called "Gnatrol," it is applied as a weekly soil drench for three consecutive weeks to control successive generations of fungus gnat larvae. Like other forms of Bt, it is not harmful to the environment and it lasts indefinitely on the shelf.

 What do YOU do about fungus gnats?

We swear a lot. We try to be grateful they aren't whiteflies. We use them to improve our hand-eye coordination, trying to catch them in midair. We hunt them down just before watering, very slowly and carefully lifting each pot to see if there are any under there we can squash with a finger. If they get bad enough, we will set out some yellow sticky traps or give the plant a dose of Gnatrol.

Beyond that, we just consider them a fact of life.

Oh, yes. We never kill a spider. We just say to it, "All right, Charlotte, why don't you go and eat a fungus gnat or two?"

The greatest advantage we have here, bug-wise, is our winter weather — most outdoor insects cannot overwinter here.

In milder climates, whiteflies can be a real problem in the garden. Here, they are mostly found inside. If you have whiteflies, they came from a greenhouse or from somebody else's house.

Only two other bugs pose a threat to houseplants in this area: aphids and spider mites. They, like whiteflies, are sucking insects. The first damage you would probably notice is a yellowing of leaves. Spider mites' damage looks like a pattern of tiny dots. If aphids or whiteflies are the culprits, the yellow areas are larger. The plant may live for a very long time with these bugs, but it will not thrive. The affected plants gradually lose leaves until they are unattractive, bare stems with tufts of leaves at the end.

If you find these insects right away and deal with them, the plant will probably recover, so check your houseplants each week to see what kind of creature may have taken up residence.

Whiteflies are highly recognizable because they really are white and they really do fly around. Most people know what aphids look like, but may not realize they come in a variety of colors and some have wings, while others don't.

You may not see spider mites unless you have very good eyes. Check for them by looking for their webs in good, strong light. They are not the lacy webs regular house spiders leave in your corners, but dense mats of webbing, usually in the angle between the stem and the leaf.

Treatment for all three of these pests is the same. First take the plant to the sink and wash it thoroughly with plain water. Not only will you wash off the bugs currently living there, you will also help to rehydrate the foliage. Humidity is usually low in our houses in the winter. If your plant is too big to be bathed in the sink, trundle it into the shower and wash it well there.

With spider mites, if you can run lukewarm water over all the leaves and stems twice a week for two weeks, that may be all you have to do.

Next, find the plant a new location right away. Spider mites in particular attack plants that are too hot or too dry, or both. If you can't move it to a more favorable environment, you could mist it, although that can be a messy proposition.

Whiteflies and aphids will require more attention. Insecticidal soap is the best invention to come along for plant lovers in a very long time. After washing the plant, spray it with a half-strength solution of insecticidal soap.

You may have a favorite recipe for using dishwashing liquid in a plant spray, but we prefer to spend the money on a formula especially for plants.

The chemical composition of detergents does not necessarily remain constant. What worked fine for you last year may kill your plants this year.

There is no reason to use anything that will harm you, your pet or the environment, but you do have to stay with the insecticidal soap program. Spray the plant twice a week for two weeks and once a week for two more weeks. Then watch it very carefully and spray again at the very first sign of a bug.

If your plant has a heavy infestation before you discover it, your best bet may be to dispose of it quickly. If it's an heirloom passed down from your great-grandmother's day and you can't bear to part with it, go ahead and control the insects, then take cuttings to restart the plant.

Remember that insects attack unhealthy plants much more often and more successfully than healthy ones. You may discover that you can't grow certain plants in your house unless you are willing to fuss over them a lot. But if you can keep your plants happy, you won't have much trouble with bugs.

 I have scale on some houseplants I can't bear to throw away. Is there anything I can do about it?

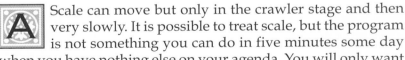 Scale can move but only in the crawler stage and then very slowly. It is possible to treat scale, but the program is not something you can do in five minutes some day when you have nothing else on your agenda. You will only want

to embark on it to save a special plant you can't bring yourself to discard. Incidentally, orchids, palms and citrus seem particularly susceptible to scale.

There are two types that affect houseplants — armored scale and soft scale. Don't let the names fool you — soft scale shells are harder than the armored variety. The individual suckers can be scraped off a plant stem. With armored scale, the soft-bodied insect stays on the stem when you remove the shell. The soft scale comes off right along with its shell. The soft scale emits honeydew and the armored one doesn't.

The first thing to do is inspect the plant thoroughly and see if it might be possible to prune away portions afflicted with scale. If scale is concentrated on a branch or two, you might try a little judicious pruning. As with all insect infestations, you have only two choices — throw the plant away or deal with the bugs. They are not going to leave voluntarily.

Also, all bumps on a plant stem are not scale, so scrape gently to see if the bumps come off.

Before you start any treatment, remove any scale already on the plant. Try using a cotton swab dipped in rubbing alcohol or use a fingernail, toothbrush, or the dull edge of a knife. If you don't take the old ones off, you might think the numbers are increasing, rather than decreasing, as you go along, since you will be taking off a lot that are no longer alive.

The swab and alcohol will work on the young stages of hard scale and on the soft-bodied types. Try that first and see how many you get. Soap sprays and oil sprays are also effective treatments, but the spray is a bit messy. Take the plant somewhere, spray and let it drip before putting it back.

Scale are most susceptible to soaps and oils when the organisms are at the crawler stage. Watch the plant carefully, checking daily with a hand lens — when first hatched, the scale may be too small to see with the naked eye. They are little round or oval things. Once you see the beasties moving, start swabbing or spraying with insecticidal soap or oil spray.

Scale, like aphids, like a high nitrogen level in their host plant so cutting down on nitrogen fertilizer will help the plant's chances.

Fortunately, scale is not the most common pest of houseplants and though it is difficult to deal with, it is not hopeless. Still, the easiest thing to do is to get rid of the plant that has it.

If you don't, make sure a plant affected by scale does not touch any other plants. Scale does not have a flying stage which limits its movement between plants. Until you know that all scale is gone, be sure the infected plants are not within touching distance of other plants.

Set up a contagious ward if at all possible, to quarantine unhealthy plants. When working with your houseplants, handle the healthy ones first to avoid spreading scale or other pests with your hands or fingernails.

 A friend gave me a grape ivy and some of its leaves are turning brown. Is there anything terribly wrong? How should I care for it?

 The first thing you should know is that grape ivy is not an ivy at all. Its botanical name, *Cissus rhombifolia,* is from the Greek for ivy, but it is no relation and got its name because it climbs and has tendrils like ivy. It is native to the West Indies and northern South America.

Your leaf browning could be perfectly normal, but if it continues or increases, it is probably due to over- or under-watering. If only the tips of the leaves turn brown, it is most likely caused by dry air.

Grape ivy is really not very fussy. It likes more moisture than regular ivy, so don't allow the soil to dry out. As with any houseplant, don't let its pot stand in a puddle. It can tolerate some direct sun, but will probably do best in good, indirect light.

Since it is a climber, you can hang it and let it trail down, or give it the support of a branch or a couple of stakes and let it climb up. You may have to encourage it to grow in the right direction.

Don't be afraid to prune any branch that is going some-place you don't want it — pinching it back will make the plant branch and become bushier.

Don't worry if any new plant you bring into your home shows signs of unhappiness. They have a whole lot of adjusting to do. It may have just come from a greenhouse with much more light than you have; it may have been given chemicals you will never inflict on it, like growth regulators, or it may be new to its pot. It will take a couple of weeks to settle in.

When you get a new plant, learn what you can about how it grows in the wild and try to give it conditions similar to its natural habitat. Climbers, for instance, do not grow in full sun because in nature they grew with bushes or on a tree.

Try to give the new acquisition the amount of water and the temperature you think it will like. Some spots in your house are cooler than others. Plants don't react very fast, so give it two weeks — then if it doesn't seem happy, you can move it or change its schedule.

If you can't find a place where the plant is happy and it dies on you, don't say, "Oh, dear, I have a black thumb." Say, "It doesn't like this house," and get yourself another kind of plant.

Why do the leaf tips of my prayer plant always turn brown?

 Around here, that happens to a lot of houseplants. In winter, the air is too dry. The roots may be just fine, but the rest of the plant is not. It helps somewhat to group plants together so they can share the moisture. You can mist them if you have the time, but mist dries so quickly that it needs to be repeated two or three times a day. You could put a cool-air humidifier near your plant.

It could be that the potting soil is either too wet or too dry. Unfortunately, the symptoms are exactly the same and only you can judge that. A plant doesn't even have to be *generally* that way—sometimes getting too dry even once will make leaf tips brown.

Also, a prayer plant is very sensitive to soluble salts in water. Areas with high fluoride get brown tips on plant leaves, and some fertilizers are high in soluble salts. Try giving the plant only organic fertilizer, like half an inch of compost every three months. Let it leach out, then scrape it off into the compost bucket and put on new. Or use a slow-release, organic fertilizer.

Or toss the prayer plant in the compost bin and start over with a plant with which you are more compatible. That's one of the advantages of a compost pile—you never really have to throw anything away. You just give it a chance to come back in a different form. Who knows what its next incarnation might be?

When you get a new plant, the instructions probably say it likes well-drained soil and advise you to keep it evenly moist or to allow it to dry out between waterings. This is not all that helpful.

What is meant by well-drained soil is that the dirt needs big pores—air spaces. So don't use garden dirt. Its pores get plugged up. Use potting soil, which contains coarse sand and/or perlite. They help the air space problem.

The roots must have air. Water plants from the top because as water drains down, it takes fresh air to the roots. A plant with no air in its soil is like you breathing into a paper bag. You could probably stay alive, but might not be healthy. It's not the ideal situation.

Wet soil in a pot is a habitat that toxin-producing organisms appreciate. Beneficial bugs, which change ammonium in the soil to a form the plant can use, cannot live in soggy soil. More houseplants are harmed by too much water than by too little.

There are lots of ways to decide how often to water, but how long it has been since the last time is not a good one. Many things can affect watering intervals. Has the temperature been higher or lower than usual? Is the plant drinking more because it's blooming?

You can tell a lot by feel. An educated finger is the best gauge of whether a plant needs water. Feel half an inch down in the soil. Feel the foliage. With practice, you will be able to tell when it needs a drink.

Plants in pots without drainage holes require extra care. Even when the soil is dry on the surface, the dirt at the bottom may still be quite wet. These plants will not require watering as often as those in pots with holes.

Perhaps the easiest method for undrained containers is to pot the plant in dry soil, then water it from a measuring cup to see how much it takes. Thereafter, give it half that amount when you water. If you aren't sure if it is too wet or not, lay the pot on its side for one or two minutes and see if any water runs out.

 When I water my philodendron, water fills the saucer, but the plant looks like it's drying up. What's the matter?

 It probably is drying up. Most potting soils have a high percentage of peat moss, which is very slow to absorb water. If it has been allowed to dry out, the water will run right through without being taken up. That's why you don't mulch with peat moss — it acts like a tin roof.

If the soil seems to be pulling away from the sides of the pot, the water is running down the sides and out the bottom without wetting the dirt.

In either case, the answer is to give it a good soaking. You can water it until its saucer is full and leave it for about six hours before emptying the saucer. Or you can put the pot in a sinkful of warm water for 10 minutes or so. Give the pot a squeeze or the soil a poke and see if any air bubbles rise, indicating that it still has room for more water in there. Then allow the pot to drain, and empty the saucer after a reasonable time.

Always water houseplants with water of room temperature or a little warmer. Not only is warm water more readily absorbed by the soil, research has shown that watering with cold water can damage root hairs.

Determining Light Levels

We have read about a neat little way to measure your plants' light levels without tools of any kind. You don't have to guess whether a plant is in low, medium or high light.

Put a piece of white paper where the leaves are — or where they would be if a plant was sitting in a particular location. Hold a book one foot away from the paper toward the light source.

If it is hard to distinguish a shadow on the paper, it is a low-light area, receiving between 25 and 75 footcandles.

If you see a definite shadow, but the edges are fuzzy, that's medium light — between 75 and 150 footcandles.

If the shadow has a sharp, distinct edge, you have a high-light area with more than 150 footcandles.

My three African violets all had large, flat leaves. They didn't bloom much, but were healthy plants. A few months ago, the new leaves began coming out small and curly. The old leaves have died. I thought they might need new soil, so I re-potted them a couple of months ago. The plants are multiplying, but the leaves are staying small and curly and there are no blooms. What is wrong? I fertilize them regularly and they are not sitting in water.

 You can't keep an African violet going without doing something to it—re-potting, starting new ones, etc. Since you have taken care of the soil and fertilizer and seem to be watering correctly, the other things we would suggest as sources of the plants' problems include light, age and insects.

We suspect that the small size of your new leaves may just be a symptom of age. The old leaves die as the plant ages and the plant tends to get stemmy. The plants seem happiest with their first rosettes of leaves near the soil.

African violets are very picky about light. In the middle of winter, with the short days, they may not be happy in the same place they were perfectly content in August. They are usually pleased in an east window or in filtered light 3 feet or so from the window. If your plants haven't been moved, their smaller leaves may be just a result of shorter days.

If the leaves are just curly at the edges, don't fret. However, if they are distorted, it is a different matter. Our first thought is bugs. Get a good, strong hand lens and look carefully at the back of the leaves for mites. The distortion could be caused by cyclamen mites which are hard to get rid of. We would recommend delivering the whole plant to the compost bin immediately if you find mites, and getting yourself some healthy new violets.

The fact that your plants aren't blooming may be the result of their reproduction—they don't bloom as much when they are multiplying. Cut off the plantlets, leaving just one. If age is part of the problem, re-potting may not do as much for a plant as cutting off the offsets. You can root them, and the new babies may produce blooms faster than a re-potted old plant.

The bloomless state also could be because the plant has not yet had time to get pot-bound. Violets bloom best when they have run out of root space.

If you want to save a parent plant that has developed a "trunk," cut off the main stem and trim off the extra length, then place it in a pot of potting soil, rooting medium or vermiculite, where it will grow new roots.

While rooting African violets, it is necessary to keep the humidity high. Something clear like plastic bags or sweater boxes can be used to create a miniature greenhouse. Just don't let the fuzzy leaves touch the plastic. Keep your little plant nurseries out of direct sun, or you will steam-cook the poor things.

 After a long stretch of sub-zero temperatures, I am worried about winter injuries to my trees and shrubs. Is there anything to be done to minimize such injury?

 You are not really more likely to get winter injuries in a colder-than-average year. These injuries are caused when temperature changes are abnormal in any direction. Tough weather, in itself, doesn't increase injury.

Plants originally grown in this area survive better than ones started elsewhere. For instance, a ponderosa pine grown locally will be tougher than one shipped in from Portland. The plants make small adaptations to the climate, although the changes are not big enough to make a different subspecies.

An unusually mild fall may prevent plants from being ready to enter dormancy when the first cold spell hits. Dormancy for woody plants is not an all-or-nothing thing. They move into and out of dormancy gradually.

One reason many plants are able to survive our winters is their ability to move water out of their cells and into the area between cells. The moisture left within the cells is then a more concentrated sugar solution and acts as an antifreeze.

The reverse is also true. A warm spell late in winter, when a plant has met its chill requirements, may cause it to break dormancy and leave it susceptible to the killing frost of the next cold spell.

Chill requirements are very specific. The length of time required varies between species, but the temperatures must be between 32 and 48 degrees Fahrenheit to count as chill requirement hours. Most woody plants (trees and shrubs) can tolerate temperatures to 40 degrees below zero, but any time after their chill requirements are met, they are ready to break dormancy. They gradually become able to tolerate less and less cold, even though they do not leaf out until air and soil temperatures are suitably warm.

Once plants start moving out of dormancy, the antifreeze goes away and the water begins moving back inside the cells, where a cold snap could freeze it and burst the cell walls. A plant can only make this water-transfer switch once in a season and cannot reverse the process if it jumps the gun the first time that the weather warms.

With fruit trees, you must consider not only their temperature tolerances, but also how early in the spring they bud out. If their blossoms come on early, the trees may live quite happily but may not produce any fruit because the flowers have frozen.

On the other hand, some long-season fruits bloom late and make nice fruit, but aren't ready for dormancy by the time cold hits. In that case, the tree dies. Plants with low chill requirements could be finished with it by Christmas, and thereafter any little warm spell could convince them to start leafing out. Plants with high chill requirements—like 1,200 hours in the temperature range mentioned—do well here.

Several winter-injury problems can affect plants. The most common here is sunscald, or southwest injury. It happens, especially to young or thin-barked trees, when the daytime sun warms the bark and thaws the fluids inside, only to have the temperature plummet as soon as the sun goes down. Prevention depends on shading susceptible trunks.

Give your young trees a chance to get hardened up by wrapping the trunk with tree wrap or heavy brown paper, by painting the trunk with white latex paint or by leaning a board against the trunk on the southwest side. In areas exposed to a lot of wind, it is a good idea to nail two boards together at right angles and lean that against the tree. If you have a lot of trees to protect, the fastest way may be to paint the trunk white to reflect the heat.

Black heart, frost cracking and, in conifers, brown patches are also winter injuries. All have been discussed by Montana State University professor George Evans in an Extension Service newsletter.

Black heart occurs when an early fall cold spell kills live tissue directly under the bark. Check for it by cutting away a sliver of bark and looking for a black layer underneath. You can help prevent black heart by cutting back on water in the fall and by not pruning in late summer.

In frost cracking, deep cracks through the bark and into the wood are caused by a big and sudden temperature drop. It is more likely to happen in trees 4 inches or more in diameter and the tree usually heals itself, Evans said.

Brown patch in conifers happens when a winter has more than the usual amount of clear, windy days. The foliage is desiccated, but because the ground is frozen, the tree's roots cannot replace the lost water. It usually occurs on the southwest side of a tree, but can happen on whatever side your prevailing winds come from.

If you have experienced this phenomenon, you can try to prevent it in the future by soaking the conifers right after the leaves drop from the deciduous trees and before freeze-up. Some winters, you may need to water your evergreens again.

Some people have found anti-transpirants, sprays that form a wax-like coating on the leaf or needle surface and hold in water, can help, but the verdict is not yet in. If you keep having problems with a particular conifer, it would probably make sense to take it out and try a different kind.

For any shrub or tree, mulching in the fall and winter helps prevent injury by moderating any huge temperature swings and holding moisture in the soil. It is done not to keep the roots from freezing, but to keep them from thawing at an inappropriate time.

For heaven's sake, don't run out in late winter and start cutting off twigs and branches you think are dead. Wait and make sure the wood is really dead. You probably will be pleasantly surprised — your plant just may leaf out late.

As soon as it gets a little warmer, pruning season will be here for all deciduous trees (except those with positive root pressure, like sugar maples and birches, which will "bleed" to death). Although pruning evergreens early doesn't hurt them, the optimum time for trimming them is when new growth is light green.

 My neighbor is out trimming his shrubbery — is this really the right time?

 If your neighbor is trimming summer-blooming shrubs and deciduous trees, his timing is perfect. These plants can be pruned at any time during dormancy, but not when temperatures are below 18 degrees, because cuts of frozen branches will not heal properly.

Spring-blooming shrubs like lilacs, forsythia and flowering almond must be pruned right after they bloom to avoid removing buds that will produce the next season's flowers. The flower buds on summer-blooming shrubs do not form until after they break dormancy.

Exceptions to the rules for pruning deciduous trees are maples, birch and walnuts, which have high sap pressure. This pressure, which allows the tapping of sugar maples, also causes pruning cuts to continue to "bleed," and cuts do not heal right. These trees must be pruned just after their leaves fall, as they enter dormancy, and before winter cold.

As a rule of thumb, do not prune a tree until two years after it is planted. Pruning for desirable shape is best done in the tree's third through fifth years.

There are several reasons, other than shaping a tree, for pruning it. To a limited extent, pruning can keep the size of the tree under control. It is useful in preventing problems like crossed branches that can rub, cause a wound and invite disease. Pruning fruit trees encourages more abundant fruiting. You also prune to prevent the tree or shrub from becoming too dense because the plant will be healthier if light and air can get to all leaves. Of course, you remove all diseased and dead branches.

When pruning, it is a good idea to dip your pruning tool in alcohol or a 10 percent bleach solution. This is absolutely necessary when dealing with diseased tissue.

The "Brooklyn Botanic Garden Bulletin" reports on a study, done at the University of California at Davis, of solutions for disinfecting pruning shears. The tests proved that 10 percent solutions of Lysol and Pinesol were as effective in pruning for fire blight as were alcohol and bleach. Alcohol and Lysol, the report says, do not cause blades to rust.

When pruning any branch coming out of the main stem, you need to leave the branch collar. This is the ring-shaped lump at the base of the limb and is really part of the trunk, rather than the branch. If you cut this collar, you wound the trunk, and it may take two or three years to recover. This may not be as pretty as a flush cut, but experts now recommend leaving the collar.

Another alteration in expert opinion in recent years is not to use pruning paint to cover your cuts. Sealing the cut prevents it from drying properly and also captures any microbes that were around at the time.

Understanding the basic structure of a tree helps you decide which branches to prune out. As a branch grows, the bark collar forms in the crotch between the branch and trunk. If the branch angle is wide, there is plenty of room for this extra bark. But if the angle is small, the bark is forced to crumple up in the limited space, making a thick layer on top of the branch. Not being living tissue, the bark provides no support for the branch, but it pushes the branch away from the trunk, weakening it.

If a narrow-crotched branch is one you really want to save for the shape of the tree, you can put about a half-cup of sand in a plastic bag and tie it on the branch near the end. The added weight may be enough to gradually bring the branch down, expanding the crotch angle.

So today is the right day and now is the right time to prune and you are standing, shears in hand, in front of the tree, but you can't bring yourself to cut anything off. Pruning seems so — well, so permanent.

There are two basic facts that can help work up your courage:

1. Trees and bushes grow only from the tips — it's the only part of the branch with the cells that can grow. A branch grows from the last bud. All the buds behind it on the branch remain dormant or grow very little.

2. Pruning stimulates growth. Any time you prune, you encourage the tree to grow more and faster than it otherwise would.

You may be pruning to remove entire branches — ones that are dead or diseased or too crowded or growing in the wrong direction. This is called a "thinning cut" and is made at the base of the branch, just outside the bark collar.

You may also want to cut off just part of a branch to fix the shape of the tree or bush. This is called a "heading cut" and is made no more than a quarter-inch past the last bud you want. This bud then becomes the terminal bud — the one that grows.

Branches should all be growing from the trunk out. Thin out any that are growing toward the middle. Also, if branches are too thick in the center of the tree or shrub, sunlight cannot reach them. Fruit trees need more thinning than shade trees, generally speaking, because the fruit on inside branches needs plenty of sun to mature. Shade trees make leaves in there, but don't have to make fruit.

With fruit trees, you also need to get rid of the water sprouts. These are the vertical, aggressively growing branches that do not fruit—fruit grows on horizontal branches, not vertical ones. Cut water sprouts all the way back to the bark collar.

An exception to this is when a tree has lost a good branch or it needs a branch in a certain place to improve its shape. You can make a horizontal branch out of a water sprout by making a heading cut just past a bud that's pointing in the direction you want the branch to grow.

Before making any heading cut, consider the direction you want the pruned branch to grow. Buds on top of the branch will grow up, those on the left will grow left, right to the right and those on the bottom of the branch will grow down. It is more important to make your cut just past a bud that will grow in the right direction than it is to have the cut exactly the distance you want it from the trunk.

All kinds of trees have a basic, natural shape. Consider the shape of your tree—does it have anything sticking out where it doesn't look good? Does it have a hole or a flat spot that needs to be filled? Prune your tree to enhance its natural shape.

With shrubs you are usually dealing with multiple trunks. If the shrub is too thick or has old wood at the bottom, you can cut out one-fifth of the trunks every year, which gives you a five-year rotation of new growth. (This does not include all the little skinny sprouts at the base, which you can remove all at once. If you want the shrub bushier, you can leave some of the small sprouts.) Prune other branches with heading cuts where desired.

I have just bought a house that came complete with rasp-berry patch, and the bushes look like they need pruning. How can I tell which canes to cut and how far back?

 The canes that bore berries last season are dead. They will be dull gray with patches of peeling bark. The live canes that will bear this summer will be a bright red-dish- or yellowish-brown and will have a green layer just under the bark.

Cut the dead canes out entirely and trim the live ones back to a height of about 4 feet.

However, unless you are particularly anxious to spruce up your raspberry patch immediately, the easiest thing to do is wait. They don't have to be pruned right now and if you wait until the buds swell, you can see for sure which canes to cut. Just see that you finish pruning before the bushes leaf out.

 Is it time to get the bulbs I planted for forcing out of cold storage yet?

 It could be. If they have grown a potful of roots, they are ready. The eight-, 10- and 12-week times we gave you in the Fall section are minimum times, however, and it is safe to leave your pots in their cool, dark place until they have sprouts 5 inches long, as long as they are not allowed to dry out completely. Having grown in the dark, the sprouts will be very pale. Put them in indirect light—inside a north window, if pos-sible—until they have a chance to produce some chlorophyll. Then treat them just like the ones you bring out unsprouted.

Bulbs being forced want lots of sunshine but cool tem-peratures. They would be absolutely delighted with 12 hours of sunlight, with daytime temperatures in the 60s and in the 40s at night. This is impossible to get in the house in winter, but try to get as close to that as possible. Think about the weather they would be blooming in outdoors. At least see that they get cooled off at night.

Keep the pots moist, but do not allow them to stand in a puddle. They won't drink much until they are growing well and the buds start to swell. As winter progresses and the bulbs approach the time they normally bloom, they will force faster. Once the flowers start to open they don't have to be in the sun all the time and can be moved to the middle of the dining table or wherever you will be able to enjoy your winter blossoms.

When your bulbs are through flowering, banish them to a place in the house where they can be ugly. Keep watering and fertilizing them as with any houseplant. When all the foliage has turned yellow, water them less, keeping them barely damp. As soon as the ground thaws in the spring, you can plant them outside. They may not grow more leaves this year, but they'll bloom again, either next spring or the year after.

The basic rule is to force a bulb only once. In forcing it into bloom early, you have called up most of the reserves it had built up. It has had only a small amount of soil to work with, temperatures were not exactly right and the roots were all cramped up in the pot.

Q I've been spending a few frigid evenings curled up with a lapful of seed catalogs and thinking about spring. There are so many varieties of the same vegetable available, and prices can vary from catalog to catalog. How can I judge which to get and which catalogs to patronize?

A If you've been happy with the seeds you have been using, quit reading. But if you want to do more experimenting with plants for short-season climates, there are a lot of small seed companies out there. Try several and compare results.

If you have trouble with your seeds germinating, don't automatically take the blame yourself. Ask if it could be cheap seed. If no germination rate is given, it's not necessarily bad seed, but you have the right to be suspicious.

One of the best ways to save money when you sell seed is to buy cheap seed and sell it for the same price as expensive seed. The people you buy seed from are very seldom the ones who grew it. None of the big companies grow any of their seed. Some of the small firms grow part of theirs and if they are honest, they will tell you that.

Probably (but not certainly) all of one variety offered in a catalog came from one grower. You can't grow spinach and have it pure if there is another variety grown within a mile or so of it.

Some companies guarantee the quality of their seed. You can feel safe if the germination percentage is shown in the catalog or on the seed packet. We feel very growly about people who aren't up-front with nice, honest gardeners.

We don't know of any of the big seed companies that have not been bought out by conglomerates whose only interest in gardening is the bottom line. Their seeds on the store racks have not been shipped for your climatic conditions.

The best seed is that which you can buy for your geographic area. The good catalogs tell you the conditions under which the variety thrives best and which diseases it is resistant to.

It is possible to get seed where none is viable and absolutely nothing grows. It is also possible to get seed where nothing in the package is what you thought it was. Failure of your seeds does not necessarily mean you are a failure as a gardener.

Molly has had experiences with both the above situations. One year she eagerly sent off for seeds of a flower she had not grown before. When none germinated, she checked into it and found that seeds of that plant must be planted immediately after harvesting and that if they dry, they die. The seed company in all probability knew this was the case, but they sold the seed anyway. One year the broccoli Molly planted grew up to be cauliflower.

There is a continuing question among gardeners about

open pollinated vs. hybrid seeds. "We need open pollination to keep up genetic stock," say some, "and anybody can grow plants to seed." Well, anyone can do it except in a place like Montana.

Because of our short season, there are very few things — maybe the earliest lettuce and radishes — that will produce mature seed before frost. But if it matters to you, seed packages that don't say it's hybrid are open-pollinated.

Besides the plethora of seed catalogs arriving in the mail, the annual crop of articles is coming out in gardening and home-type magazines, telling who has catalogs, how to send for them and recommending some above others. You need to be aware that some of these articles are written in ignorance by people who know nothing about gardening, and others are paid for by the companies mentioned in the story.

If you have not had experience with a particular catalog, we suggest that you talk to gardening friends for recommendations or warnings. You can also start slowly, ordering a few things from different places and seeing how you like the results produced by each. In any case, do keep track of which seeds came from which company.

One word of advice: If you order your seeds from catalogs, do it early. It definitely pays to beat the rush. It really is wise to order as soon as you can. Some plants and seeds are in short supply, and orders are processed in order of receipt.

 The seed catalogs are pouring in and everything looks and sounds so good. How can one ever choose just one or two varieties of each vegetable from the dozens that are offered?

The only real question is whether a variety will grow well here in Montana.

Other than that, it's strictly a matter of personal preference, which may include considerable trial and error and some recommendations from gardening friends.

The most important information about a vegetable variety is its "days to maturity."

There's nothing magic in this number and nowhere is it chiseled in stone. It is merely the grower's best guess of how long it will take the seed to produce a crop under ideal conditions.

We rarely, if ever, have those ideal conditions. So if on June 1 you plant a corn with a 62-day maturity, don't expect to go out to the patch and pick sweet corn for your company dinner on August 1.

For all warm-weather crops, those that do not tolerate frost, you cannot safely plant until early June. Maybe in a sheltered garden you could get away with mid-May. The old rule used to be Memorial Day — Decoration Day to old-timers. Therefore, you must select varieties with 80 days to maturity or less. The earlier, the better. This gives the plants not only the best chance to survive and produce an edible product, but also their best chance to thrive.

For cold-weather crops which tolerate some frost, the number of days to maturity doesn't matter as much.

Lettuces rated at 53 days and 73 days will probably do equally well. They like the summer weather we have here.

When a radish says 27 days, you can probably count on having radishes in 27 days.

The same is true for carrots and lettuce, but not for tomatoes and beans. Our growing season is not their idea of "ideal conditions."

There is no way to say, "This variety will be best for you." Much depends on your soil and your microclimate. Your soil may be different from your next-door neighbor's and your front yard may have a different microclimate from the back. These things you will have to learn from experience.

One year does not a true test make. Last year's failure may be this year's roaring success. Our rule of thumb is to give it three years before giving up.

I'm not a very experienced gardener, but I'd like to try a few new things. I'm overwhelmed by the varieties of vegetables available. Could you recommend a few that I could expect to do well?

 If you are a beginning gardener, don't start with demanding things such as cauliflower. And, for heaven's sake, don't plant the entire packet of zucchini seeds — for reproduction, zucchini are the rabbits of the vegetable kingdom.

When choosing among varieties of any vegetable, opt for the earliest one that sounds good to you. Not all types enjoy our cool nights and would give up before they got started. Others need a growing season longer than ours to mature before frost.

If you have never gardened before in your life, you can be successful with lettuce. You can grow any kind of lettuce you want here. Leaf lettuce is the fastest, head lettuce and romaine the slowest.

If you plant some lettuce every two weeks all summer, you will have a constant supply of salad greens. If you like spinach in your salads, we think Bloomsdale Long-standing gives the best results here.

The cole crops — cabbage family — are cool-weather crops that do well here. Early Jersey Wakefield is a very good early English cabbage, but early cabbages do not store well. If you want to grow one to store in the fall, be sure the seed packet says it's a storage cabbage. Be prepared — your cabbages will probably be bigger than the package says they will. They tend to grow large here.

Whatever kind of sweet corn you want to grow, remember that the standard varieties with SU genes are the earliest. Those with SE (sugar-enhanced) or Sh2 (super-sweet) genes are later and do not do as well in cool climates.

We have two favorite peas. Green Arrow is not early, but it is very disease-resistant and produces an average of 10 peas per pod. Daybreak is a very good early variety, although it does not produce as many peas per pod.

If you want early beans or have had trouble growing beans on your garden site, grow bush beans. Montana Green, developed at Belgrade, is a good variety for here. A variety called Label is a filet bean — very long and thin with excellent flavor. Royal Purple beans have good flavor and are interesting because they turn from purple to green when cooked.

For something special in potatoes, try yellow ones such as Yukon Gold or Russian Banana. Although they have been around for a long time, they haven't been on the home-garden market very long. They do well here and taste wonderful.

Among winter squash, we have found that Sweet Mama, a buttercup type, does better than any others we've tried.

If you have grown lettuce for a while, you may have run across a French variety called Merveille des Quatres Saisons (translation: Marvel of Four Seasons). It is halfway between a leaf and bibb lettuce, halfway between green and red. It is an heirloom variety with a great flavor; it is very tender, one of the earliest to produce in the spring and does not bolt in summer. If you can't find it in your seed catalog, look for Continuity lettuce. It's the same variety, renamed for reasons known only to the translator.

With onions, the first criterion is to choose long-day types. Short-day onions are for southern areas like Georgia.

Almost any radish will grow well here, but you might try a European variety just for its interest.

If you plant melons, choose the earliest variety, plant in rich soil in your sunniest location on a south slope, sheltered from the wind, hold your mouth right, and cross your fingers all summer.

In edible-pod peas, we prefer the true Chinese types like *Ho Lohn Dow*. The pods stay thin and the peas do not mature. They are true snow peas, as opposed to the sugar peas, which can be eaten through maturity.

Snap peas are a cross with beans and the less said about them, the better. One dinner guest decided to call them "peans" because they included the bad qualities of peas and beans, but none of the good.

Of course, we heard from a reader with an entirely different opinion on snap peas:

"I'm writing to refute your denunciation of sugar snap peas, or "peans," as you called them. Last spring our then 4-year-old daughter Sarah Ann picked up a variety called 'Sugar Ann.' (We think she was attracted to the name.) They grew beautifully and tasted even better. We ate them in salads, sauteed, steamed and by the handful while weeding the garden. We blanched and froze several bags and have been eating them all winter. They will definitely be a part of our seed order this year and every year to come."

We're sure there are many other fans of sugar snap peas. There are probably a lot of folks out there who enjoy stewed okra or rutabagas in their soup and we don't like those, either.

Many of the things upon which we pontificate are pretty firmly based in science or personal experience, but some of the stuff we say is just a matter of personal taste and needs to be taken with a grain (or two) of salt. We are definitely in favor of anybody growing anything that appeals to them and deciding for themselves whether they like it and whether it works in their gardens.

 If you are ordering seed for a specific variety, why should it matter whether it comes from Idaho or South Carolina?

 It is not really a question of where the seeds are shipped from. What matters is where the seed was grown. You need to consider more than just a plant's variety in choosing seeds for our northern climate.

We, in our sparsely populated area with its harsh climate, are not the primary market for companies that distribute nationally. You can't be absolutely sure where seeds were grown — they may well not have been produced in the United

States. About the only control you can exert is to buy your seed from a company growing its seed especially for cool climates.

For those with a serious absorption with seeds, there's a new book out that has been getting good reviews. It's "Breed Your Own Vegetable Varieties" by Carol Deppe, a geneticist with good credentials. It could help you understand what you're likely to get if you cross-breed plants, how to go about it and why it might be worth it.

 I put my tuberous begonia away for the winter, leaving it in its same pot. It has already started to wake up. This isn't supposed to happen, is it?

 This is most unusual. No self-respecting tuberous begonia even thinks about waking up in winter. Your begonia might possibly need re-potting. Wet the soil and turn it out. If all you see is roots, give it a larger pot.

If it doesn't require re-potting, it may just not be paying attention to what a proper tuberous begonia should do. Sometimes what a plant is doing doesn't apply to the rules as if it were following directions in a recipe. Growing plants is not like making chocolate chip cookies.

The snow is finally off my flower beds. Should I be doing something out there this early?

 This is the time to start paying attention to your perennials. The mulch should come off now. It has served its purpose, which was to keep the plants frozen through the winter. But now that the weather is warming, it will be keeping them warm, which you don't want. You want them to become accustomed to the temperatures going back and forth past freezing and not to come out of dormancy sooner than absolutely necessary. Some may already be poking through.

Molly is reminded every March of why she plants primroses. At the beginning of March the plants all look utterly brown. After a week they all have little green centers. By mid-March they are almost totally green; most of them have bud clusters and a couple are already in bloom.

If you haven't cut off your perennials' dead growth from last year, do that now. If you are going to do the chore gradually, start with the toughest ones, like columbines and iris, because they green up earliest.

In cutting back any perennial, aim for two inches above the ground. At that height, you will not injure the crown, but the new growth will quickly cover the old stems. It is very time-consuming to remove old growth once the new stuff comes in.

The ground is not thawed enough yet to divide things, but it's a good time to look at your plants and decide what you want to divide when the time comes. If a perennial has formed a doughnut shape, it is time to split it. Dividing early is the best plan because it gives the plant a good, long growing season, but don't dig them up if the ground is mud. It is hard on the soil structure.

If you had any problems with diseases or infestations of insects last season, remove any litter the plants dropped on the ground around them. If not, there is more to be gained from leaving it than removing it. Or you could remove it and return it later as mulch.

The general pig-headedness of gardeners occurred to us one week as we discussed growing stuff.

Georgianna was slightly resentful of the time and effort she had to put in on the poinsettia in her living room when she went to California for Christmas and discovered the plants there growing rampant and blooming profusely up past the eaves of the houses.

Molly had just returned from a visit to her sister in the Los Angeles area, where she found her sister bemoaning the fact that she couldn't grow good raspberries.

Serious gardeners in Montana go to great lengths and invest heavily — both financially and emotionally — to get azaleas to bloom. Yet in England, where azaleas do beautifully, gardeners build elaborate raised and rocky beds to grow plants native to our mountains.

It is probably just human nature to want to accomplish the difficult, if not the impossible. Any old body can grow petunias and green beans. To distinguish oneself as a gardener, one must rise above the ordinary.

Having the most succulent sweet corn or the most vibrant verbena is all very well. But to have orchids opening in your office or brussels sprouts burgeoning in the backyard — these are the accomplishments from which status accrues.